Ancient Rome in the English novel

A study in English historical fiction

Randolph Faries

Alpha Editions

This edition published in 2024

ISBN : 9789366389554

Design and Setting By
Alpha Editions
www.alphaedis.com
Email - info@alphaedis.com

As per information held with us this book is in Public Domain.
This book is a reproduction of an important historical work. Alpha Editions uses the best technology to reproduce historical work in the same manner it was first published to preserve its original nature. Any marks or number seen are left intentionally to preserve its true form.

Contents

PREFACE ....- 1 -
I Definition of the Field..- 2 -
II Genesis of the Novel of Roman Life ....- 10 -
III Principal Lines of Development of the Novel of
 Roman Life from 1834 to the Present Day..........................- 20 -
IV In Conclusion ....- 78 -
FOOTNOTES ....- 81 -
Bibliography ....- 84 -

PREFACE

For some time I have felt the need for a satisfactory definition of the "classic" novel,—a definition which should include novels of value, and exclude innumerable works of fiction of little or no value. The want of such a definition was evident not only from the vagueness with which literary historians have referred to the "classic" novel, but also from the fact that other students seemed to consider as such any work of fiction using Greek and Roman names. For a definite selection of theme, I am indebted to Dr. John Cooper Mendenhall, of the Department of English of the University of Pennsylvania, whose generous advice I wish to acknowledge most gratefully, and whose fine sense for literary form has been an inspiration to me in my work. I wish to express my most sincere appreciation for many helpful suggestions, to other members of the Department of English, whose lectures have provided, I feel, a background for this study. I have also to thank Dr. Eugene Stock McCartney, of the University of Michigan, for freely providing me with a list of titles, which has materially aided me in making complete my list of all works of fiction dealing with ancient Rome.

RANDOLPH FARIES, 2D.

UNIVERSITY OF PENNSYLVANIA, MAY, 1923.

I
DEFINITION OF THE FIELD

It is my purpose in this study to show the use which the English historical novel has made of the rich and abundant material furnished by the life of ancient Rome. In doing this I shall trace the genesis of the novel of Roman life and its development, with special emphasis upon elements of permanent value. As an aid to a clear perception of this latter point, I shall give a carefully selected list of the best novels of Roman life, pointing out their claims to greatness. At the end of my study will be found a complete list of all books which make any pretense of presenting Roman life in the form of a novel.

Since ancient Rome is often associated with ancient Greece in classical study, the question may arise as to why novels dealing with life in ancient Greece are excluded from consideration here. The answer is that comparatively few such novels have been written. The author who writes of ancient Rome has at his disposal abundant materials from which he may construct a novel; he who writes of the life of ancient Greece finds his sources somewhat more limited. Another consideration which has influenced authors is that modern life is more immediately related to the life of ancient Rome than to that of ancient Greece. The classic period of Greek history was of comparatively short duration, and, in one sense, the life of ancient Greece lost its identity even before it was absorbed by the life of the Roman empire; while the life of ancient Rome made itself felt in the most remote parts of the widely extended Roman world. We must give full recognition to ancient Greece for her contribution to the world's culture, yet admit that her influence upon the world today has been overshadowed by the power of Rome. The story of Rome's power, rather than that of the culture of Greece, has found expression in the modern novel.

A novelist who writes of ancient Rome may deal with any period of Rome's history, from the traditional date of the founding of the city to the time at which Rome ceased to be the head of the western Empire. A convenient division is made when we speak of (1) Rome before the Empire, (2) Rome under the Empire. Pre-imperial Rome has furnished the inspiration for comparatively few novels. Since, however, some of these are of great merit, it will be well to examine certain portions of Rome's early history with which they are connected. One excellent novel[1] deals with prehistoric Italy and the first faint beginnings of Roman things. Immediately following the legendary period of her existence, Rome was chiefly concerned with struggles with her Italian neighbors; these struggles have inspired no great novel in English, though several good books for boys have been written about them. The desperate conflict between Rome and Carthage offers material for a novel of strong appeal. But the stirring times of the later Republic present the best field for the novel of pre-Imperial Rome.[2] The period of the Empire, however, when Rome was undisputed mistress of the world, is the time which has appealed to most of the novelists who write of ancient Rome.

The number of novels or of books masquerading as novels, which make some use of Roman life as a background, is large; many of these purport to be what they are not. So, if one reviews even a small portion of the entire number, it becomes obvious that many, if not most of them, are neither literature nor anything else of value. There is one class of novels, whose purpose is not primarily to represent life in ancient Rome, but to make other work attractive by the addition of artificial coloring. The use of such superficial aid in a novel nearly always reveals the absence of any serious purpose. This lack of seriousness is well illustrated by the work of Sir Rider Haggard in such[9] pseudo-historical novels as *Cleopatra*, and *Pearl Maiden*. A novel which seems to come a little closer to being truly "historical," is *Unto Caesar*, by the Baroness Orczy; but, on closer examination, this book is found to belong to the "artificial" class we are discussing. It makes use of a few striking facts in the life of Caligula, but the deep significance of these facts and of its quotations from the Bible, is entirely lost, owing to the light and cheap sentimentality which pervades the whole volume. A further illustration of pseudo-sanctity is seen in the recently published novel of Dr. Burris Jenkins, *Princess Salome*.[3] When fantastic and improbable stories are woven around historical characters in a novel; or when facts of deep historical significance are made to aid the novelist in a frivolous pretense to serious work; the result is sure to be a work of small merit. Novels in which a supposed setting of Roman life merely conceals inferior work and makes it appear attractive, will not be considered in this study.

There is a second class of books whose chief purpose is not portrayal of life in ancient Rome, but rather a kind of religious propaganda. They set forth in the form of fiction, some story inspired by the records of the New Testament, or taken from the chronicles of Church history. Not all of these books are to be called novels, but they have been produced in large numbers, and have a significant relation to the kind of novel we are considering. Many stories of the early Christians, particularly of martyrs in the arena, may be told in such a way as to portray the life of Rome very inadequately. They often ignore the pagan point of view, and in most cases deliberately misrepresent it. In such a book as Cardinal Wiseman's *Fabiola*, (1855), the Emperor and his soldiers are mere abstract representatives of power and evil; while the Christians artificially personify virtue and martyrdom. The work of Mrs. J. B. Peploe Webb is well represented by *Pomponia*,[4] a moral story of supposed religious experience. Many such books have been written since

1850, and published by religious publication societies. They usually present merely a stereotyped analysis of the character of some Christian martyr, while a smattering of history is used to blindfold, rather than to enlighten the reader. A novel which is truly to portray the life of ancient Rome may well include within its scope the life of the early Christians, but we shall not consider those books which deliberately present either Christians or pagans in a false light.[5]

Of special interest to the teacher of history are juvenile stories of Roman history, written for boys in fiction form, since many of these truly portray a part of the life of ancient Rome. It must be observed, however, that books for boys are subject to some limitations not placed upon novels written for their elders. Such well-known authors of books for boys as the Rev. Alfred J. Church and G. A. Henty have recognized that they must present a hero who will appeal especially to boys, and that this hero must have adventures illustrating schoolbook history. In Church's book *Two Thousand Years Ago*, Spartacus is represented as a truly noble figure, while in *The Young Carthaginian*, Henty makes Hannibal the real hero. But the technical hero in each of these books is an idealized youth, who rushes from one exciting adventure to another. Moreover, both Church and Henty tried to make the study of history instructive, by introducing into their fictions for boys favorite incidents of the history books. The result was that their novels for boys became too heavy with history. The general criticism may also be made of such books for boys, that they make too much use of the life of the soldier and the gladiator, to the exclusion of other elements in Roman life. There is, however, a fairly accurate portrayal of Roman life, from a teacher's point of view, in some books for boys; such books are not to be confused with religious stories of the Sunday-school type, and have a definite connection with our subject.

After excluding novels which use Roman life merely to make other work attractive, or as an artificial background for religious instruction, we find that there still remain a considerable number which attempt to portray Roman life, but are unsuccessful. The novelist may fall short of his aim through lack of scholarship, through want of appreciation of the essential worth of his subject, or through sheer inability to appeal to his readers directly. There may be found on the shelves of public libraries, many novels, in which the characters have Roman names and are supposed to live in ancient Rome; but many of these novels do not really portray the life of Rome at all. Some of them feebly essay to imitate books of established reputation, and prove to be very poor imitations. The present study will be chiefly concerned with those novels which make a serious portrayal of the life of ancient Rome for its own intrinsic interest.

We are dealing then with that form of the historical novel which portrays the life of ancient Rome. The historical novel may be defined as that form of the novel which makes use of historical characters and events as an integral part of the story. Ample support may be found for this definition in the always candid words of Sir Walter Scott, the first really great English historical novelist, in his introductions to the *Waverly Novels*. In the *Prefatory Letter* to *Peveril of the Peak*, he has the anonymous "Author of Waverly" say, "A poor fellow, like myself, weary with ransacking his own barren and bounded imagination, looks out for some general subject in the huge and boundless field of history, which holds forth examples of every kind,—lights on some personage, or some combination of circumstances, or some striking trait of manners, which he thinks may be advantageously used as the basis of a fictitious narrative, ... invests it with such shades of character as will best contrast with each other—and thinks, perhaps, he has done some service to the public if he can present to them a lively fictitious picture, for which the original anecdote or circumstance which he made free to press into his services, only furnishes a slight sketch." Again, in the introduction to *The Abbot*, Scott says, "I naturally paid attention to such principles of composition, as I conceived were best suited to the historical novel;" and this when he has just made it clear that the choice of a famous historical character[6] as subject is the readiest, though the most difficult, way to instant success. In a note to the introduction to *The Abbot*, he says, "There occur in every country some peculiar historical characters, which are, like a spell or charm, sovereign to excite curiosity and attract attention, since every one in the slightest degree interested in the land which they belong to, has heard much of them, and longs to hear more." The importance of a theme based on famous historical events, to an historical novel, is attested by Scott in his introduction to *Red Gauntlet*. Here he says, "The Jacobite enthusiasm of the eighteenth century, particularly during the rebellion of 1745, afforded a theme, perhaps the finest that could be selected for fictitious composition, founded upon real or probable incident." In the introduction to *Woodstock*, Scott says, "Nothing, indeed, is more certain, than that incidents that are real, preserve an infinite advantage in works of this nature (historical novels) over such as are fictitious." Not every novel which tells a story of the past is a true historical novel; it must make some vital use of historical characters and events if it is to be considered truly historical.

But the function of the historical novel is not to teach history as it is taught by the schoolbook. It is rather to aid the reader to a sympathetic appreciation of history in the broader sense,—the history that reveals the life of the past with all its significant relations to the life of the present. As Scott explains, "The love of knowledge wants but a beginning—the least spark will give fire when the train is properly prepared; and having been interested in fictitious adventures ascribed to an historical period and characters, the reader begins next to be anxious to learn what the facts really were, and how far the novelist has justly represented them."[7] Moreover the aim of the best historical novels is not to *escape* the present and carry the reader back to the past, but to bring the present and the past face to face,—in short, to portray life as it exists, and always has existed. "The passions, the sources from which (sentiments and manners) must spring in all their modifications, are generally the same in all ranks and conditions, all countries and ages; and it follows as a matter of course, that the opinions, habits of thinking, and actions, however influenced by the peculiar state of society, must still, on the whole, bear a strong resemblance to each other."[8] An historical novel is great,—when it *is* great,—because, in its study of the life of the past, it displays the same qualities that give value to the life of today. The true test of greatness in an historical novel may be defined at once, as the test of its success in portraying the past with realistic effect.

With this test in mind, I have reviewed all novels of Roman life which a most thorough search has brought to light, asking the question: What degree of success do they attain in portraying the life of Rome with realistic effect? This was done in order to obtain from a multitude of novels of different degrees of merit, a standard representing the best and most significant work that has been done in the novel of Roman life. Judged according to this standard, the best and most representative novels of Roman life are those which appear in the following list. I have made this list with the intention of basing upon it my deductions concerning the achievement of English and American authors in the field of the novel of Roman life.

A. IMPORTANT NOVELS OF ROMAN LIFE

Valerius, a Roman Story: John G. Lockhart, (1821)

The Epicurean: Thomas Moore, (1827)

Sathaliel, the Immortal: George Croly, (1829)

The Last Days of Pompeii: Sir E. G. Bulwer-Lytton, (1834)

Zenobia: William Ware, (1836)

Attila: G. P. R. James, (1837)

Probus—later called *Aurelian*: William Ware, (1838)

Julian, Scenes in Judea: William Ware, (1841)

Antonina: Wilkie Collins, (1850)

Hypatia: Charles Kingsley, (1853)

The Roman Traitor: Henry Herbert, (1853)

Callista: John Henry Newman, (1855)

The Gladiators: G. J. Whyte-Melville, (1863)

Ben Hur: Gen. Lew Wallace, (1880)

Marius the Epicurean: Walter Pater, (1885)

Darkness and Dawn: Archdeacon Frederic William Farrar, (1892)

Gathering Clouds: Archdeacon Frederic William Farrar, (1895)

The Sign of the Cross: Wilson Barrett, (1897)

Perpetua: Rev. S. Baring-Gould, (1897)

Domitia: Rev. S. Baring-Gould, (1898)

A Friend of Caesar: William Stearns Davis, (1900)

Vergilius, a Tale of the Coming of Christ: Irving Bacheller, (1904)

Psyche: Walter S. Cramp, (1905)

Veranilda: George Gissing, (1904)

An Heir to Empire: Walter S. Cramp, (1913)

Behold the Woman: T. Everett Harré, (1916)

The Unwilling Vestal: Edward Lucas White, (1918)

Evander: Eden Philpotts, (1919)

Andivius Hedulio: Edward Lucas White, (1921)

Pan and the Twins: Eden Philpotts, (1922)

The above list represents my choice, based upon reasons indicated, of the most important novels of Roman life. The process of selection may be carried still further, however; and, using the same standard as before, I have chosen from this list a dozen novels which stand out above the rest, and are to be considered the absolute best among novels of Roman life. This more select list is as follows:

1. *The Last Days of Pompeii*: Bulwer, (1834)

2. *Hypatia*: Charles Kingsley, (1853)

3. *The Gladiators*: G. J. Whyte-Melville, (1863)

4. *Ben Hur*: Lew Wallace, (1880)

5. *Marius, the Epicurean*: Walter Pater, (1885)

6. *Darkness and Dawn*: F. W. Farrar, (1892)

7. *Domitia*: S. Baring-Gould, (1898)

8. *A Friend of Caesar*: William Stearns Davis, (1900)

9. *Vergilius, a Tale of the Coming of Christ*: Irving Bacheller, (1904)

10. *Veranilda*: George Gissing, (1904)

11. *Andivius Hedulio*: Edward Lucas White, (1921)

12. *Pan and the Twins*: Eden Philpotts, (1922)

These twelve novels are of permanent value. None of them are either obsolete or obsolescent. But for the benefit of those who raise the cry: "Of what practical good is anything which does not satisfy the present popular taste?" I wish to make an interesting comparison. After deciding upon the above list of twelve novels, I came upon *A Classified List of the Best Modern Novels that are in ACTIVE USE in the Public Libraries of the United States*. This was compiled with infinite pains by Mr. William Alanson Borden, not with any scholarly purpose, but with a view to ascertaining what novels were *most read*. While his list of novels of Roman life stops at the year 1910, it can be seen that it closely corresponds with the one I have just given. His list of novels of Roman life, written in English, is as follows:

The Last Days of Pompeii: Bulwer

Hypatia: Charles Kingsley (given under "Alexandria," not "Rome")

Ben Hur: Lew Wallace

Marius, the Epicurean: Walter Pater

Domitia: Baring-Gould

A Friend of Caesar: W. S. Davis

Vergilius: I. Bacheller

*Aurelian: William Ware

**The Son of the Swordmaker*: Opie Read

**The Sign of the Cross*: Wilson Barrett

Of the novels marked with an asterisk, *Aurelian* was excluded from my list, as being somewhat too "gloomy" for modern taste. *The Son of the Swordmaker* and *The Sign of the Cross* were novels of widespread, but transient popularity. This may be said also of *Vergilius*, but to a less extent. The three novels on Mr. Borden's list which I have marked with an asterisk are the only ones which do not appear of my list of the twelve best. On the whole, Mr. Borden's list of the best confirms my own, and the twelve novels given in the first of the two lists will receive our chief attention.[9]

II
Genesis of the Novel of Roman Life

We have indicated what novels are to be given an important place in the field of the novel of Roman life; but before considering so fully developed a form as Bulwer's *Last Days of Pompeii*, let us see what the soil was, from which such a form grew. Since the novel of Roman life is a definite variety of the historical novel, we must first consider the origin of the historical novel as such. The true historical novel, it has been said, portrays the past with realistic effect. Since the time of Scott, historical fiction has in the main followed the example which he set in his historical novels, and it is largely due to this fact that some authors have attained notable success in portraying the life of the past with realistic effect. Before Scott's time historical romances existed, often taking such a form as to point directly toward Scott's work, and even attaining much of his success in such a realistic portrayal of life. Yet in 1785, Clara Reeve had somewhat arbitrarily said: "The Romance, in lofty and elevated language, describes what never happened, nor is likely to happen."[10] This definition does not seem to allow that the historical romance had achieved realistic effect at all, and so does not fairly represent the facts. But it must be remembered that the definition applied not only to the historical romance, but also to another form of the romance, which has been called the "Gothic" romance. While Scott's work in the historical novel is, in a sense, a continuation of the historical romance, the "Gothic" romance better represents the school of fiction which Scott supplanted. For this reason it seems better to dispose of the "Gothic" romance before we discuss more fully the early development of the historical romance.

The "Gothic" romance begins with Horace Walpole's *Castle of Otranto* (1764), which has no real historical background, though the events are supposed to have happened in the twelfth or thirteenth century. Walpole had built a supposed "Gothic" castle, which he called "Strawberry Hill," and the castle became a part of the "Gothic" romance. Walpole supplied this form of the romance with its familiar supernatural machinery, its ghost, creaking doors, subterranean caverns, etc., which need not be described here. It is well to note, however, at this point, that Scott, who adopted some of the saner elements of the Gothic romance, used the supernatural as something inseparable from many of the real Scotch characters, whom he described. Clara Reeve's *Champion of Virtue* (1777), later called *The Old English Baron*, is to be noted, since it contains both Gothic and historical incidents. The Gothic romance was further developed by Mrs. Radcliffe, "Monk" Lewis, and others. Mrs. Radcliffe especially influences Scott and the later novel. She develops the description of those aspects of nature which later impressed Byron, and is undoubtedly the creator of the "Byronic hero." Her

"Schedoni" is in all essentials Byron's "Lara," an individual apart from other men, with a certain nobility of his own and a "vital scorn of all." Lord Byron and his school reproduced certain elements of the "Gothic" romance, and in turn had an influence on the novel. The "Byronic hero" and the Byronic passion for the terrible aspects of nature will appear in the novel of Roman life and assume a prominent position. The Gothic romance continued to exist after the time of Mrs. Radcliffe; it took various forms, such as the detective story and the fantasy, as well as the tale of terror, with its superstitious elements. Down to 1850 it remained the fashion for almost any novelist to arouse his readers from time to time by a narration of marvelous or terrible events. The Gothic romance served to show that literature is not merely utilitarian; even in its wildest forms, it retained certain marks of the realistic novel, and added testimony to the fact that realism and romance are, after all, inseparable. While not making a thorough study of mediæval times, it pointed the way for Scott, in dealing with this period of the past. It also had an important effect on the novel of Roman life in its formative stage, as will be seen.

The so-called "Oriental" romance is really a development of the Gothic. It originates with the work of William Beckford in *Vathek, an Arabian Tale*. This was a consummate piece of art of its kind, and had a tremendous influence on the writing of the time. Beckford built in Wiltshire, an enormous mansion with mysterious halls and galleries, in which he tried to realize his dreams of Oriental luxury. *Vathek* was written in French and published in France in 1787. It was translated from the French manuscript by Samuel Henley, an English scholar, and published in London in 1786, without Beckford's consent. Among other things, *Vathek* is noteworthy for its descriptions of Oriental "magic," and its employment of what may be called the "labyrinth motive." This motive appears in the stories of all ages, its classic example being the story of the labyrinth at Crete (which was, perhaps, really a palace). It is used in some of Scott's novels (notably *Woodstock*), and in many novels of Roman life, in which the characters have to pass through a series of dark and intricate passages in the catacombs at Rome, or cut in the rock near some city of Egypt. The use of Eastern magic is sometimes combined with this motive and so appears in more than one novel of Roman life. The influence of *Vathek* and the "Oriental" romance, considered apart from other varieties of the Gothic romance, on the novel of Roman life, is considerable.

The true historical romance is even more important in its relation to our subject. In tracing its development before Scott, the first important example is found to be *Longsword, Earl of Salisbury, an Historical Romance* (1762), attributed to the Rev. Thomas Leland, of Dublin. This romance reproduces feudal scenes such as are found in Shakespeare's historical plays, and anticipates many of the elements of Scott's historical romances. While the story is told, however, with the detail of an authentic historical document, it lacks historical perspective. *Longsword* stood alone for a time, except for Clara Reeve's *Old English Baron* (1777): this romance of Clara Reeve's combined historical and "Gothic" incidents, as already mentioned, and had the effect of adding historical details to the customary castle and ghost in the Gothic romance. But in 1783 appeared *The Recess*, which is the first of a series of historical romances down to Scott, and marks a closer approach to the true historical novel. Its theme is the same as that of *Kenilworth*; and may owe something to Shakespeare's *Anthony and Cleopatra*, as *Kenilworth* does. Many of this series of romances do, in fact, derive their history from Shakespeare's historical dramas. They show an increasing attention to the facts of history, which culminates in the romances of Jane Porter. Jane Porter's imaginative treatment of history far surpasses any previous attempts. Her *Thaddeous of Warsaw* is almost wholly historical, though deficient in characterization and plot; while in preparing to write *The Scottish Chiefs* she actually visited the places which she intended to describe.

Jane Porter may fairly be given the credit for developing the use of historical background to a point of perfection, and so preparing the way for Scott. Moreover, Scott, with all his romantic imagination, owes something to the "Gothic" romancers, who preceded him. What, then, did Scott himself add to the historical novel? Bearing in mind our definition of the historical novel, two points are to be considered essential in our answer: He added (1) the realistic sketch of the manners of the past; (2) characters who are real beings, who represent human nature. These two points are suggested by Scott in his General Preface to the *Waverly Novels*. It is clear that while he is speaking of two circumstances which led him to finish *Waverly*, his words are to be applied to the whole series of the Waverly novels. The circumstance which led Scott to undertake to reproduce faithfully the manners of the past was his completion, in 1808, of the unfinished romance of the antiquarian, Joseph Strutt. This romance was called *Queen-hoo-Hall*, and described the time of Henry the Sixth; it attempted to give a "pleasing representation of the manners and amusements of our forefathers." (Strutt's Preface.) Scott perceived that the reason for its failure was the author's "rendering his language too ancient, and displaying his antiquarian knowledge too liberally"; and resolved to avoid the mistake "by rendering a similar work more light and obvious to general comprehension."[11] Strutt showed that the historical novelist should attempt an exact reproduction of the past; but Scott further made it clear that the manners of the past cannot be reproduced with realistic effect, if the author relies solely on antiquarian knowledge, or if he fails to bring his description home to readers of the present, in terms intelligible to the majority of them.

Of even greater importance to the historical novel was Scott's determination to do for the people of Scotland, what Miss Edgeworth had done for the people of Ireland,—to bring before his readers real Scotch people of all ranks and conditions of society, to portray human life in his pages. Scott is especially a realist when dealing with characters taken from lowly life; but his realism is not confined to lowly life alone, as some critics would have us believe. His great historical figures, it is true, are often given romantic and literary treatment; but even they do not lack human touches, and in any case, a proper balance is maintained by including characters who are human enough. What has made Scott's novels deserve to endure is his faithful representation of human nature. The same thing could be said of any great historical novel, whether it deals with England or America a few years back or with the remote times of ancient Rome. Scott's plan in writing the historical novel, was to create imaginary characters, with all the attributes of real human beings, and to place them in an historical background, containing a few historical characters. This plan, in the main, has been followed by successful historical novelists since his time,—including those who write of Roman life,—and seems best adapted to portraying the life of the past with realistic effect.

It may now be asked when Roman life was first drawn upon in what may be termed "historical fiction"; whether any evidence of this is to be found before the period when Scott set alike the standard and the fashion in that form of writing. It must be remembered that classic subject-matter has taken a large place in many forms of English literature, though it would be out of place to give examples here taken from other forms of literature than fiction. Not to mention the very early translations and reworkings of mediæval legends on classic subjects, it is well to recall that Chaucer uses classic subject-matter abundantly, and that his *Troilus and Cressida* approaches the modern historical novel in nearly every way, though it is written in verse. If we are looking for an early presentation of Roman life in a form leading toward modern prose fiction, we must turn to the allegorical quasi-historical romances of the seventeenth century. One of them which may be claimed for England is the *Argenis* (1621), of John Barclay. Barclay, who was born in France, of Scotch father and French mother, lived for a time in England and finally went to Italy, where he wrote the *Argenis* in Latin. It describes important historical characters of his own time, but under classic names. Its scenes are placed in classic countries and the story is told in terms of Roman life and custom. A marriage is performed in a temple dedicated to Juno and Lucina, high priests perform the ceremony, and the bridal party honor Hymen and Apollo. Barclay opened the way for a series of French romances which were much in vogue in England. This led to the formation of literary societies, to one of which Roger Boyle belonged. His *Parthenissa* (1654), is another historical allegory, like Barclay's; it confuses several great Roman wars, bringing Hannibal and Spartacus into the same scene.[12] Such romances show something of Roman life in the form of fiction, but are far removed in some ways from the modern historical novel; and it will be best for us to return to the time of Scott, and search for a portrayal of Roman life in the fully developed form of the historical novel.

A. THE FIRST TRUE NOVEL OF ROMAN LIFE

The first significant attempt in English to portray life in that period of the past during which ancient Rome flourished, in the form of the modern novel, appears in *Valerius, a Roman Story*. It is not to be regarded as a mere coincidence that its author was John G. Lockhart, a son-in-law of Sir Walter Scott. The year 1821, in which it was first published, was also marked by the appearance of *Kenilworth* and *The Pirate*. In *Kenilworth*, Scott owed much to Shakespeare's *Antony and Cleopatra*, a play with a classic subject. And while Scott was showing how the past could be presented in the novel, it was altogether natural that Lockhart, a classical scholar, should decide to make use of classic material in this form. Classic times had furnished abundant material and true inspiration in other forms of writing. Though *Valerius* is not a great novel, it has certain elements of permanent value. It is a very thorough and scholarly piece of work, well-balanced and accurate in detail. Its characters, Christian and pagan, are fairly well-done, and its scenes represent, with some degree of realism, the amphitheatre, the crowded streets of Rome, the law-court, and the suburban villa. While Christianity is not overemphasized, the martyrdom of Thraso, an old soldier, who has become a Christian, is described with real pathos. The story is laid in the time of Trajan, who is justly represented as a popular ruler, and not a cruel tyrant. The customary use is made of Pliny's correspondence with Trajan, regarding treatment of the Christians. The book is not without humor, though its general tone is serious and it contains a little too much philosophy. It was republished in 1835, the year after Bulwer's *Last Days of Pompeii*. *Valerius* may fairly be considered the first novel of Roman life. This seems to be implied by Cardinal Newman, who mentioned it many years later in his preface to *Callista*.

B. THE INFLUENCE OF "VATHEK" ON THE NOVEL OF ROMAN LIFE

In 1827 Thomas Moore published *The Epicurean*. This is to be classed as a romance, and is akin to and inspired by the work of William Beckford in *Vathek, an Arabian Tale*. Moore's *The Epicurean* takes from *Vathek* its descriptions of Egyptian magic, and its use of the "labyrinth motive";[13] these are things which appear in a modified form in Bulwer's *Last Days of Pompeii* (1834). *The Epicurean*, however, in spite of its fantastic nature, contains realistic descriptions of the persecution of the Christians in Africa, under

Diocletian, and a contrast of Christianity with a pagan system of philosophy (Epicureanism). While its story does not take the reader to Rome, *The Epicurean* represents life in Greece and Egypt under Roman rule, and must be considered a step in the genesis of the novel of Roman life. It represents new elements which are not found in *Valerius*, but appear frequently in later novels of Roman life. *Vathek*, which Moore says was his model, has been mentioned as an "Oriental" romance, this kind of romance being a variety of the "Gothic"; and when certain elements of the "Oriental" romance appear in novels of Roman life of this early period, it is more logical to ascribe their existence to the influence of *Vathek* than to say that they merely come from *The Epicurean*. But we have to consider at this point not only the influence of *Vathek* as a thing entirely separate from other literature of the period; for the hero of *The Epicurean* is the "Byronic hero," already mentioned in connection with Mrs. Radcliffe and Byron. The terrible side of nature, which had appealed to these authors, appears in *The Epicurean*, combined with Egyptian "magic"; the hero in passing through the mysteries of initiation is surrounded by roaring winds and rushing waters. Thus it appears that *The Epicurean*, while it falls far below the first rank,[14] is important, because it shows the effect which the Gothic romance, with its various developments, was having on the early novel of Roman life.

C. THE INFLUENCE OF THE "BYRONIC ROMANCE" ON THE NOVEL OF ROMAN LIFE

In 1829[15] was first published a romance by George Croly, called *Salathiel, a Story of the Past, the Present and the Future*. It enjoyed wide popularity and was favorably reviewed both in England and America; and was issued at different times with variations of the title, such as *Salathiel, the Immortal, or the Wandering Jew*. Finally it has been revised and republished posthumously, in 1901, under the title of *Tarry Thou, Till I Come, or Salathiel, the Wandering Jew*. This last edition was published in somewhat elaborate style with copious introduction and appendix, and beautifully accurate illustrations, by Mr. T. de Thulstrup. Especially noteworthy is the introductory letter of General Lewis Wallace, who, in making his remarkable choice of the six greatest English novels, includes "*Hypatia*, and this romance of Croly's." While his choice of the "six greatest" is unusual, he gives very sound reasons for his support of *Tarry Thou, Till I Come*. General Wallace, who is best known for his *Ben Hur*, also wrote *The Prince of India*, in which he handles the theme of the Wandering Jew, describing the wanderings of the Jew in Moslem times.

Croly was born in 1780 in Dublin and died in 1860. In *Salathiel* he follows the school of Byron and Moore, which was dominant in his youth. The style of the book is marked by a warmth of coloring, and Croly excels in his handling of powerful situations. The character of Salathiel, surrounded by perpetual gloom, and displaying a proud aloofness from other men, has much in it of the "Byronic hero." The terrible aspects of nature are also presented with telling effect, and much in the Byronic manner throughout the story; Croly is at his best in this sort of work in a chapter, which has been given the title *The Wanderings of a Mind Diseased*, and which represents the reality of Salathiel's imaginary trials. In this chapter the description of a volcanic eruption suggests a similar description made by Bulwer in *The Last Days of Pompeii*, a few years later. The scene of *Salathiel* does not open in Rome, but from the very start, the reader feels the intensity of the Jewish hatred for Roman power. The degenerate Roman governor of Judea, Gessius Florus, is well portrayed in his capacity of extortioner and tyrant. He sends Salathiel to Rome, and at this point in the story we are given in a brief space many of the important elements in any novel of Roman life which deals with the time of Nero. There is the prisoner, calmly condemned to a death of torture, while the Emperor feigns practice on the lyre; then the fire at Rome is powerfully described, and when it is over, the blame for it is attached to the Christians; the Christians are put to death by torture in the amphitheatre, or torn by wild beasts; they are made to serve as living torches in Nero's gardens; and finally the persecution ceases. Though his name is not mentioned, the martyrdom of St. Paul is told in such a way as to portray his indomitable spirit and courage in the face of death.

The scene of the remainder of the story is again laid in Judea, and the story of events culminating in the capture of Jerusalem by a Roman army, is taken from Josephus.[16] In this part of the book things Roman are best represented by the figure of the Prince and commander, Titus, and by the soldiers and officers of the Roman army. The divisions of the Roman army are described with great realism, recruited as they are from almost every tribe and nation under the sun. The fierce struggles between Roman and Jew outside of the walls, give opportunity for some of the finest pictures of desperate fighting to be found in any novel. The "labyrinth motive," one of the oldest motives in story telling, is used a number of times in the latter part of *Salathiel*; it is used with much ingenuity in the description of his entrance into the fortress of Masada by a secret underground passage; and again, when, escaping from prison, he finds he has blundered upon the secret rear entrance of the pirates' cave.

Salathiel is a truly great romance, in which the exalted language is suited to the grandeur of the theme. While "romance" is the proper word to describe the book as a whole, individual passages exhibit a realistic effect which far surpasses anything in the pages of *Valerius* or of *The Epicurean*. Moreover, it is sound in its historical basis, for Croly was a man of genuine learning, classic[17] and otherwise. On the other hand, it must not be supposed, because he was a curate, that he wrote *Salathiel* with any intention of spreading religious propaganda. The scene in which the Christians, imprisoned and awaiting crucifixion, exhibit their supreme faith, is one of tremendous significance; but this could be said of many other scenes in the book. Even if it were not a story of absorbing interest, *Salathiel* would deserve a high position in fiction, for its illustration of great principles in life, and its powerful revelation of eternal truths.

D. THE NOVEL OF ROMAN LIFE IN A FULLY DEVELOPED FORM

In 1834 was published Bulwer's[18] *Last Days of Pompeii*, which probably has been as widely read, and for as long a period as any other historical novel. Men still live who consider Bulwer among the greatest of English novelists; and if one were to select only one book for which he is especially remembered, I believe The *Last Days of Pompeii* would have equal claims with such a novel as *The Last of the Barons*, to which critics usually assign a higher place. *The Last Days of Pompeii* was a new thing of its kind; it represents a new departure in the historical novel, and in the novel of Roman life. It is true that there remain in it certain elements of the Byronism, which was still so prevalent in the novel of the day, but these elements cannot merely be dismissed as defects. There is the Byronic passion for the terrible in nature, which reaches its height in the unsurpassed description of the eruption of Vesuvius, and its terrible effects. The "Byronic hero," moreover, can easily be seen in the disguise of Arbaces, the Egyptian, who is surrounded by an air of mystery, and has a lofty scorn of the common herd of mankind. Moreover, Arbaces, to secure his ends, has recourse to Egyptian "magic," the intricacy and subtlety of which had been well represented in *The Epicurean*. Such motives as these, however, have already been discussed, together with their relation to the novel of Roman life. Let us see what Bulwer added to this particular variety of the historical novel.

It will be recalled that Scott (who must be considered Bulwer's most important predecessor in the field), in writing his historical novels, always made use of historical characters and events, as well as of purely imaginary characters and events. Bulwer departed from this program, in the first instance, by reducing the number of historical events,—the eruption being the only important one. Moreover, he succeeded, with no loss of effect, in replacing the "historical" characters, which are usually necessary to the historical novel, by imaginary characters such as he perceived would be in harmony with the time he described. This omission of "historical" characters is to be accounted for by Bulwer's choice of scene. Having chosen Pompeii (and not Rome) for his scene, and finding there were no "historical" characters suitable for a novel portraying the life of this brilliant Campanian city, he decided to make up for their absence by lending an almost "historical" reality to his imaginary characters. Scott had made his imaginary characters appear to be real men and women by reproducing real men and women whom he had observed; Bulwer, in writing The *Last Days of Pompeii*, undertook the more difficult task of representing men and women who might well have lived in the times of ancient Rome,—and succeeds rather well. Around these characters he decided to weave a narrative which would reproduce exactly the life of the time,—and in this he succeeds admirably. Scott had been warned by the mistake made by the antiquary, Joseph Strutt, in a misuse of antiquarian details. Bulwer was an antiquarian of an entirely different sort; he revelled in the use of details, but in putting them into his story, made the whole conduce toward realistic effect. He had read widely in Latin and Greek literature; he climbed Mt. Vesuvius and learned all he could by actual observation, filing every detail in huge commonplace books; he studied Roman antiquities, and compared the results of his study with the manners of modern Italians. In short, he realized in his imagination the decadent life of Pompeii as it had actually been just before the eruption of Vesuvius, and reproduced it in the pages of The *Last Days of Pompeii*. While Bulwer, therefore, did not reproduce historical characters and events in quite the same way that Scott did, he makes an even more concrete use, than Scott did, of that life of the past which is not recorded in formal history. He views the past from the standpoint of the philosopher as well as from that of the student of human nature. Moreover, he seeks for permanent truths in human nature, rather than for merely picturesque elements.

The title and subject of *The Last Days of Pompeii*, was first concretely suggested to Bulwer's mind by a picture of the same title. This picture, he says in his journal, was one of a collection in the Brera Gallery at Milan, and was "full of genius, imagination and nature. The faces are fine, the conception grand." And as the author says in his Preface to the 1834 Edition, having chosen for his subject the "catastrophe, the Destruction of Pompeii, it required but little insight into the higher principles of art to perceive that to Pompeii the story should rigidly be confined. Placed in contrast with the mighty pomp of Rome, the luxuries and gaud of the vivid Campanian city would have sunk into insignificance. Her awful fate would have seemed but a petty and isolated wreck in the vast seas of the imperial sway." Bulwer therefore decided to avoid the temptation "to conduct the characters of his tale ... from Pompeii to Rome," leaving "to others the honor of delineating the hollow but majestic civilization of Rome." The last part of this quotation is especially important to us. Bulwer in his preparatory studies spent much time in Rome, as well as in the vicinity of Pompeii. While the story of The Last Days of Pompeii does not actually go to Rome, all of its important elements, save the description of the eruption, could be transferred to a story of the Imperial City. Thus Bulwer's novel not only shows that the novel of Roman life had become firmly established as a definite type, but it also points forward and shows the way for all important novels of Roman life since its time. The mingling of Romans and Italians, with Greeks and other foreigners in

Pompeii, suggests the hybrid population of Rome; the worship of Isis, and her priest, the Egyptian Arbaces, suggest not only the varied forms of pagan religion at Rome, but also the important connections of Rome with Alexandria and the Nile civilization; the early struggles of Christianity (represented by Olinthus, and his converts) with these pagan superstitions recall the even greater trials of the Christians at Rome; the witch of the crater, with her spells and incantations, reminds one of the Sibyl of Cumæ and the soothsayers who appear at Rome in later novels of Roman life. The minor incidents of Bulwer's novel and his descriptions of the manners of society also are used in novels whose scene is Rome; the banquets and revels, the life of loungers at the bath and spectators at the amphitheatre, the habits and haunts of the gladiators, the busy hum of the forum, are all things which Bulwer showed later novelists how to portray. He realized that he must not make his characters talk in the periods of Cicero, and takes without question the opinion of Scott (voiced in the preface to *Ivanhoe*), that the historical novelist should "explain ancient manners in modern language." Bulwer's method was somewhat different from that of Scott; but his purpose was essentially the same. His ideal is fairly stated at the end of the Preface to the 1834 edition, viz., to present a portrait faithful "to the features and costume of the age which I have attempted to paint. May it be (what is far more important) a just representation of the human passions and the human heart, whose elements in all ages are the same." How well he achieved his purpose and realized his ideal is amply shown in The *Last Days of Pompeii*. Writers of the novel of Roman life who have followed Bulwer have surpassed him in few respects. Their purpose must be essentially the same as his; their ideal could not be higher.

Before the close of the year 1834, *Valerius* and *The Last Days of Pompeii* are the only two important novels whose scene is laid almost entirely in or near ancient Rome.[19] This fact is attested by historians of the novel; but if one is not satisfied without hearing an opinion of an author's work expressed by one of his contemporaries, we have the tribute of Sir Archibald Alison (*History of Europe*, 1815-52, ch. V). He says in speaking of *Valerius*, "The most successful attempt which has yet been made to engraft the interest of modern life on ancient story: its extreme difficulty may be judged by the brilliant genius of Bulwer having alone rivalled him in the undertaking." If there is any other book written before 1834, which deserves in every respect the title of "novel of Roman life," I have been unable to trace it, nor do I know of any one else who claims to have done so. In considering the genesis of the novel of Roman life, one may be confident that *Valerius* first marks out its general outlines, and *The Last Days of Pompeii* establishes for it a complete and artistic form.

III
Principal Lines of Development of the Novel of Roman Life from 1834 to the Present Day

In considering the principal lines of development which the novel of Roman life has followed in its development from the time of Bulwer's novel to the present day, one fact seems fairly obvious, but cannot be overemphasized. No important novel of Roman life has been written by an author who lacks classical scholarship of a very high order. Needless to say, such scholarship implies the possession of a highly cultivated intellect, and stands far above mere book-learning or pedanticism. In a general survey of the field it very soon appears that scholarship of this kind was possessed by the great scholar and preacher, Charles Kingsley, and is finely exemplified in his *Hypatia*, in spite of what pedantic critics have said concerning his "history." After Kingsley, other great scholars, who were also preachers, made the novel of Roman life a vehicle for the presentation of universal truths. Besides such preachers, Ebers, Eckstein, and other followers of Scott in Germany,—whose classic novels constitute the most important influence from abroad on the English novel of Roman life before the time of *Quo Vadis* (1896),—showed the value of absolute thoroughness in matters of scholarship. While they sometimes were led in their careful research to place undue emphasis on minute particulars, they often succeeded in giving to their work an atmosphere of universal truth. Novelists, whose principal purpose seems to have been to tell a "rattling good story" or to present a series of gorgeous pictures of Roman life, soon came to realize the necessity of scholarly accuracy, if they would attain to realistic effect. This was true of Whyte-Melville, the author of *The Gladiators* (1863), and of General Lew Wallace, who wrote *Ben Hur* (1880), though it must be admitted that the latter was somewhat more of a scholar, and had a more serious purpose. The success of men who have made a business of scholarship speaks for itself in the more recent and really fine work of Mr. William Stearns Davis in *A Friend of Caesar* (1900), and of Mr. Edward Lucas White in *Andivius Hedulio* (1921). But the finest fruits of the true scholarly mind have ever pointed toward the intellectual, the æsthetic, the beautiful in thought and expression. The beauty of thought and expression of Walter Pater's *Marius, the Epicurean* (1885), has perhaps never been surpassed in English prose fiction. Some approach to the quality of Pater's work, however, is seen in that of George Gissing, in *Veranilda* (1904), and an even greater similarity to it appears in parts of *Pan and the Twins* (1922), by Mr. Eden Philpotts. Novelists such as these seek not merely to portray life as it appears to the average observer, but to make possible a fine appreciation of many things, which exist only for those who are seeking truth and beauty beneath the surface.

A. NOVELS OF ROMAN LIFE WHICH SHOW EVIDENCE OF THE SCHOLARSHIP OF GREAT PREACHERS

Let us consider first that phase of the development of the novel of Roman life, which is seen in novels showing unmistakable evidence of the scholarship of great preachers. A significant proportion of the limited list of the best novels of Roman life previously given consists of novels written by preachers. Now in defining the novel of Roman life, those books were excluded, which make use of Roman life merely as an artificial background for religious instruction. But it would certainly be a needless restriction to deny to the novel of Roman life, or indeed to any form of the historical novel, the liberty to present, directly or indirectly, any valuable sort of teaching. It is impossible truly to portray the life of ancient Rome, without teaching many things of lasting value. Moreover, there is a grave error in supposing that those important novels of Roman life which are written by preachers have as their sole purpose the preaching of Christianity; nor do they endeavor to portray the life of the Christians alone, and to deny a fair representation to the Pagan life which all but overwhelmed Christianity. A fairer statement of the case would be to say that preachers of scholarly attainments have been eminently fitted to write of Roman life through their study of that period of the world's history, which is marked by the formation of the Roman Empire and the beginning of Christianity. Consequently they have produced novels in which the life of the early Christians appears naturally as an essential part of the life of ancient Rome. To include the life of the Christians in the novel of Roman life is not absolutely necessary, though all of our preacher-authors have done so; but it is more natural to do so in a novel, the story of which is laid after the time of Christ, and nearly all authors of such novels have appeared to recognize this. Finally the scholarly preacher has proven to be the best qualified of all men not only to present something of the dramatic struggle between Christianity and the pagan world; but also to portray the life of Rome in such a way as to bring home to his readers universal truths far above the level of mere didacticism. Unless such truths are sensed and illustrated by an author, no portrayal of the past can attain to an entire completeness of realistic effect.

The first significant novel of Roman life by such an author, was the work of the Rev. William Ware, a Unitarian preacher of Boston, and thorough classical scholar. In 1837, three years after *The Last Days of Pompeii* appeared, he published *Zenobia, or The Fall of Palmyra*. Ware was no doubt led to write a novel of Roman times by the work of Bulwer and other novelists of the British Isles, who had done so; though in his work there is none of the Byronism which had appeared in the work of Croly, the only other preacher whose novel has been discussed so far in this study. Just what influenced Ware in his choice of title and subject is not quite so clear. As far back as

1814 there had been published in London a work by a certain Miss O'Keefe, entitled *Zenobia, Queen of Palmyra, a Narrative founded on History*. This combines slow-moving dialogue with narration of the style of a school history book, and can hardly be classed as a genuine novel. While it is fairly accurate in its history, it does not appear to be of sufficient merit to have influenced Ware in his far superior work, even if he knew of it. A much more likely supposition is that Ware was first attracted in the course of his reading by the life-story of the famous queen who dared to lead her army against the hosts of the Roman empire; he then found further encouragement to write the novel from the popularity of historical fiction and from his familiarity with the sources from which the facts of Zenobia's story are readily derived. In any case, *Zenobia*, among novels so far considered, (when published) had been equaled only by Croly's *Salathiel* in the accurate and abundant use of historical facts derived from original historical sources. Pollio, the biographer of Zenobia, Vopiscus, the biographer of Aurelian, and other historians, are accurately quoted to establish important points; and when there is evidence on both sides of a question, Ware weighs it very carefully. On the other hand, he does not make the mistake of crowding his pages with notes. These are condensed within the space of a few pages at the end of each of the two volumes.

Zenobia is written in the letters of L. Manlius Piso, an imaginary personage who is supposed to have been in Palmyra at the time of its fall, and who writes to a friend at Rome. Since the first letter describes to his friend how he left Rome, the scene may be said to open at Rome, and it returns to Rome when Zenobia has been made a captive by Aurelian. Moreover, the character of Piso is distinctly Roman, and the cruel, stern emperor, Aurelian, appears as a true Roman. The military operations of the Romans before the walls of Palmyra, and the Emperor's triumph at Rome with Zenobia as his captive, are well described. There is thus much of Roman life in *Zenobia*. Its so-called "epistolary" or "Richardsonian" style, is heavily descriptive, but the general effect is one of soundness, and the novel is impressive, not dull. In fact, *Zenobia* possesses a brightness of coloring and an atmosphere of reality which seem superior to anything in Ware's later books. While the minor characters do not stand out strongly, they are nevertheless real and human enough. Any deficiencies shown by the other characters are atoned for in Ware's presentation of Zenobia, whom the author successfully portrays as a real woman and a proud queen. Ware is also true to history in recording that Zenobia had heard much of Christianity, but did not finally decide to become a Christian. Though a preacher, he preferred to state the probable truth, rather than to change the facts for the sake of preaching. In this he points the way for other preacher-authors who followed him in writing the novel of Roman life. *Zenobia* was widely read on its first publication and attained equal success when it was posthumously published in 1869.

The success of *Zenobia* led its author to publish a sequel in the following year, 1838. This was called *Aurelian, Emperor of Rome*, when it was republished shortly afterward, and goes by that title, though its original title was *Probus*. The scene of this novel is laid entirely in Rome, and the supposed narrator speaks as though he had survived Aurelian, had seen something of the persecution of Diocletian, and finally enjoyed safety under Constantine. Like *Zenobia*, *Aurelian* is written in the form of letters; these letters are supposed to have been collected by a freedman of one of the characters. While it contains the story of a conversion to Christianity, *Aurelian* is not to be classed as propaganda of any sort. Whatever preaching there is in it consists merely of a realistic portrayal of the sufferings of the Christians under persecution. The scenes in which Christians are submitted to various forms of torture are by no means overdrawn, and the martyrdom of some of them in the arena is described in a convincing manner. Over-emphasis on the place of Christianity in Roman life is to some extent avoided by making the Emperor a more important figure than any one of the Christians. *Aurelian* is a book of one important character, the Emperor being the dominant figure. Ware's second novel may truly be called a novel of Roman life, since it portrays faithfully some aspects of life at Rome in the time of Aurelian. But even in these terrible times there were other things in the life of Rome than the persecution of the Christians; and a more complete effect would have been obtained by including some of these in the picture. The fault is not overemphasis of one element so much as the omission of others. The author was careful in his study of life at Rome, but limited that study too much to a single phase of Roman life. One of his contemporaries, Miss Mitford, in her *Literary Recollections*, said of *Aurelian*, that it showed "not a trace of modern habits or modes of thinking;" but this is a purely negative compliment. The novel does portray something of ancient Roman habits and modes of thinking; its psychology is good in the case of the Christians and their persecutors. While not making quite the same use of the larger facts of history as appears in *Zenobia*, Ware showed his scholarship in *Aurelian* especially well in his minutely detailed description of the Roman system of espionage, and of the traits of character which were exhibited in the Roman masters of the world. Though its tone is too sinister for present-day taste, *Aurelian* made a great impression in its day, and takes an important place in the development of the novel of Roman life.

Ware's third novel, published in 1841, was called *Julian; Scenes in Judea*. This is also written in the form of letters; and the story is told in the words of a wealthy young Jew, who leaves Rome, where he has been staying, and returns to his native land. *Julian* can hardly be called a novel of Roman life, since, as the alternative title implies, most of the action takes place in Judea; and it excels rather in its portrayal of the Jewish national life, than in its description of the Romans. A fine conception, however, of the grandeur and extent of the Roman Empire is afforded by the description of the travels of the young Jew. Realistic touches are added in pictures of the stately buildings of Asiatic cities and of wild animals, which are being shipped for the games in the arena. Furthermore the delineation of the Roman governor Pilate and of Roman soldiers in Judea is made with masterful strokes. But the significant thing in *Julian* in relation to the development of the novel of Roman life, is that it is the first novel approaching that type, which has for its central theme the life-story of Jesus Christ. Though it is beyond the power of any novelist to tell this story with one-half the power of the inspired narrative of the New Testament, even when feebly retold, it is of such tremendous meaning, that any portrayal of Roman life made in connection with it is sure to pale into insignificance. *Julian* proved conclusively that a novel which is intended primarily to portray Roman life, cannot make the life of Christ its central theme. The Rev. Mr. Ware's three novels were not only very popular in America and in England, but were translated into German and other foreign languages. They were very favorably received by contemporary critics. In reviewing *Julian*, shortly after it appeared, Dr. R. W. Griswold says, "The romances of Mr. Ware betray a familiarity with the civilization of the ancients, and are written in a graceful, pure, and brilliant style." No novel in America surpasses the novels of Ware in their importance in the development of the novel of Roman life before the publication of Gen. Lew Wallace's *Ben Hur* (1880).

The Rev. Ware's *Julian* has just been mentioned as an illustration of the fact that no novel, whether written by a preacher or not, can successfully portray Roman life, while making the life of Christ its central theme. *Aurelian* was also spoken of, to illustrate the more general truth that in a portrayal of Roman life in a novel, the life of the Christians should not be given undue prominence. Mrs. Webb's *Naomi* (1841),[20] is a story which begins immediately after the time of Christ, but much of the life of Christ is brought in by the words of the aged Mary of Bethany and others of His disciples who are still living. Moreover, the life of the Christians, as contrasted with that of the Romans, is given undue prominence. *Naomi* has, in fact, been mentioned in the first section of this study, and was excluded from consideration as a novel of Roman life, since it is rather a story of religious experience. It is now mentioned again to remind one that it is the first important one of a very great number of religious books that were written from this time on. In other words, the year 1841 marks, as nearly as possible, the exact point at which the story of religious instruction branches off and becomes an entirely different thing from the novel of Roman life. The Rev. Ware's *Julian* and *Aurelian* are not in any sense stories of religious instruction, but they suggested to other preachers and people interested in religious work the possibility of writing such stories. Thus the story of religious instruction was a by-product of the early novel of Roman life; but it continued to exist as a distinct form, and to have an influence in turn on the development of the novel of Roman life. It is important to bear this influence in mind, even though the story of religious instruction showed not so much what the novel of Roman life should do, as what it should avoid.

In 1853[21] appeared Charles Kingsley's *Hypatia*. This is a great novel, which in its presentation of universal truths far surpasses the stereotyped instruction of any religious tract. It is a powerful picture of the conflict between Christianity and Greek philosophy in the fifth century. Its author fairly presents the beauty of Greek philosophy, before showing that the true spirit of Christianity must triumph in the end. But Kingsley also showed the essential falsity of the teachings of the Greek schools of philosophy, which his heroine, Hypatia, represented; and he pointed out in an equally convincing way, that the Christian Church, while almost entirely shutting out spiritual Christianity, had become an organization, whose chief end was temporal power. By considering this last fact outside of its proper relation, Kingsley's enemies were enabled to wilfully misunderstand him, although those who still read *Hypatia* for its own sake are always able to understand him perfectly. In fact, the reasons which led Kingsley to write *Hypatia*, have frequently been misstated. It will be well to consider what the facts were, especially since they have an important bearing on the development of the novel of Roman life.[22]

Hypatia is, in the words of William T. Brewster, Professor of English at Columbia University, "a very decided sermon in favor of spiritual Christianity." This explains in part Kingsley's purpose in his portrayal of life in the Roman empire of the fifth century. Let it be said right here, however, that while *Hypatia* contains more preaching than any other novel we have to consider, it is entirely free from hollow didacticism. As its alternative title, *New Foes with an Old Face*, implies, Kingsley was supporting the cause of spiritual Christianity against new elements, which were assailing Christianity in the same way in which it has always been assailed. One of the most powerful of these elements, at the time when Kingsley wrote, was deemed to be the false Hellenism which was then trying to supplant Christianity in England and on the continent. This form of paganism has no uncertain connection with the Byronism, of which we have already spoken, while its tendency to exalt Greek philosophy had been beautifully expressed in Schiller's poem *The Gods of Greece*. Kingsley's desire to combat this tendency may be the principal reason why he chose for his scene Alexandria; since in this city was best represented the crisis of the dramatic struggle between Christianity and Greek civilization in the fifth century. But another important element which Kingsley was fighting,—(and critics have made the mistake of supposing it to be the only one), is represented in the tendency of the Church of England toward Rome. This movement was chiefly due to John

Henry Newman, who went over to the Church of Rome, and whose *Callista* we shall have occasion to mention later. But it is interesting to us to note that the conspiracy to Romanize the Church of England, which Kingsley combatted, centred at Oxford; and, as has since been pointed out by literary criticism, the Oxford movement was an evidence of the Romantic spirit represented by Scott. For, long before Newman went over to Rome, Scott's mediæval priest had gained the sympathy of countless English readers.[23] Thus Kingsley, who is a direct follower of Scott in the historical romance, was forced to combat the tendency of Scott's readers to identify romance and mediæval Catholicism. G. P. R. James, an earlier follower of Scott, though anything but a propagandist, had spoken of Rome in *Attila*, (1837), as the "seat of the most autocratic government the world has ever seen, republican, imperial and *clerical.*" These words contain whole volumes of criticism, and show how another writer of the novel of Roman life had identified the city of Rome with the Church of Rome. This suggests another reason why Kingsley chose Alexandria, rather than Rome, for the scene of his portrayal of the struggle between Christianity and Paganism, in *Hypatia*. Had he merely wished to portray this struggle, he might well have laid his scene in Imperial Rome, as others have done, and have achieved tremendous effect. But his opponents would have insisted on identifying the early Church *at* Rome with the Church *of* Rome, and the situation at the time forbade his allowing them the satisfaction of claiming that the triumph of Christianity is to be found only in "the Eternal Church of Rome." In *Hypatia* Kingsley in no way exceeds the limits of truth in his delineation of the faults and hypocrisy of the early Church, though his opponents could not stand the truth told of what they conceived to be an eternal and perfect thing, (the Catholic Church). His faithful presentation of life in the Roman empire, and of universal truths to be derived from a study of the past, make *Hypatia* continue to be read as a great novel which has to be considered as a thing far above sectarian controversy.

Kingsley's own idea of what he wished to do in *Hypatia* is admirably expressed in a letter to the Rev. F. D. Maurice, written from Eversley, January 16, 1851. (He writes of financial difficulties, which compel him to support himself with his pen,—how this recalls Scott!) He then says: "My present notion is to write a historical romance of the beginning of the fifth century which has been breeding in my head this two years.... If there is a storm brewing, of course I shall have to help to fight the Philistines.... My idea in the romance is to set forth Christianity as the only really democratic creed, and philosophy, above all spiritualism, as the most exclusively aristocratic creed. Such has been my opinion for a long time, and what I have been reading lately confirms it more and more. Even Synesius, 'the philosophic' bishop, is an aristocrat by the side of Cyril. It seems to me that such a book might do good just now, while the scribes and Pharisees, Christian and heathen, are saying, this people which knoweth not the law is accursed." He wished to turn from English subjects "to some new field, in which there is richer and more picturesque life.... I have long wished to do something antique, and get out my thoughts about the connection of the old world and the new; Schiller's *Gods of Greece* expresses, I think, a tone of feeling very common, and which finds its vent in modern Neo-Platonism— Anythingarianism."[24] Kingsley wished to show "the connection of the old and new" in important phases of life and thought; and incidentally that in any portrayal of life, thought must be considered an essential part of life. He succeeded admirably in this, in writing *Hypatia.*

In his desire to "show the connection of old and new," and to portray "a richer and more picturesque life," Kingsley naturally turned to the times of the Roman Empire. Why he did not select the city of Rome for his scene, has already been suggested. Nevertheless, *Hypatia* may well be called a novel of Roman life. In the first place the scene practically does move to Rome, when we follow Raphael Aben-Ezra in his travels to the immediate vicinity of the eternal city. In the scenes leading up to the defeat of Count Heraclian at Ostia, Rome's seaport, the presence of the capital of the world is felt in the background. Moreover, the scene of the rest of the story is not confined to Alexandria, but takes one to visit Saint Augustine and Synesius at Cyrene. The allusions to the powerful position which Constantinople had assumed in Church and government affairs completes the impression of the Roman empire as a loosely organized whole. A further consideration shows one that the important scenes which occur in Alexandria could, without difficulty, be transferred to Rome, and described as a part of Roman life. The brutal and licentious spectacles in the amphitheatre, the ostentatious display of the upper classes, the lawless rioting of the lower classes, who are sometimes curbed by Roman authority with unnecessary bloodshed, and much else, are portrayed with a realistic effect, which could hardly be surpassed in a portrayal of life anywhere else than in Rome itself. In the time which *Hypatia* describes, it is true, Rome was no longer mistress of the world, but there remains an all-pervading sense of her former greatness. Alexandria, though a city possessing its own distinctive characteristics, had not escaped the universal stamp of Roman influence. A few short years before Kingsley's story opens, the Goths, under Alaric, had sacked Rome, (410 A. D.), and Alexandria furnishes in some ways a better example of the many sided life of the declining Roman empire than does Rome itself. There is, in short, an abundance of "Roman life" in Alexandria.

If Alexandrian scenes in *Hypatia* could be transferred to Rome, a similar thing might be said of certain characters in the book. The most truly Roman characters are Victoria and her father, who had been a Roman officer in the force of Heraclian; these enter the story when its scene is nearest to Rome.

The armed forces of the weak Roman government at Alexandria are also typical of Rome, whether performing as gladiators in the amphitheatre, or employed in quelling a riot in the streets with brutal carelessness of life and feeling. Orestes, the Roman governor of Alexandria, is a typical Roman official, capable of thinking for himself when not intoxicated, and bright enough to admit that he is forced to be a puppet; "a poor, miserable slave of a governor," who appears to feel that his very treachery is forced on him by circumstance. Old Miriam is a sorceress of a type which suggests the sibyls and later soothsayers at Rome, by whose arts the Romans were so ready to be deceived, and whose prophecies exerted so profound an influence on the imaginations of the Romans. One of her victims is Hypatia, whose character stands out with such strong individuality as the last support of Greek philosophy in Alexandria, that it would be impossible to make her play her part in a novel whose scene was laid principally in Rome. But many of the other characters, major and minor, could be placed in such a novel without disadvantage; indeed some of them have spent a good part of their lives in Rome, when the story opens. Figures such as Arsenius and St. Augustine represent men who had seen the world of Rome, and were seeking refuge from its emptiness. The tyrannical bishop Cyril embodies a character which could have displayed the autocratic power of the Church at Rome or at any other important city of the Empire. Philammon, the real hero of the story, is the kind of character who would fit in readily in any environment and could easily be made a Roman. He is the best illustration of a fact we have mentioned before, viz., that the historical novel should contain characters who are, above all, human beings. Philammon's essentially human qualities gain the reader's sympathy at once; and as he is tempted by one doubt after another, one is reminded that the men of the past were merely human beings like ourselves. Among the Gothic invaders of the Roman Empire, old Wulf best represents those qualities which Englishmen have regarded with pride as being typical of the English race. Pelagia is a type which existed at Rome as at Alexandria. The same thing can be said of the little porter, and of all the minor characters. With characters such as these playing their parts in scenes of varying significance, Kingsley has presented a vivid panorama of the life of the time, which could only have been equalled by a portrayal of the life of Rome itself. Without an excess of detail or an undue use of the sensational, he has succeeded in emphasizing the important points in the picture, and in implying those of less importance, so well, that the life of the past is made to stand out in the clear light of present-day experience.

By portraying the life of the past in the light of universal truth. Kingsley was able to show, without stereotyped preaching, the triumph of Christianity over paganism. Greek philosophy had been appropriated by and identified with the so-called "national" religion of Rome, and had found its greatest stronghold in the Hellenistic city of Alexandria. Hypatia herself deserves to have her name made the title of Kingsley's novel. She is rightly presented as typifying the last adherent of paganism against Christianity. The strength of her character lies in the truth of her words, as compared with the inconsistencies of the monks. And it is to be regarded as an essential point in the story, that the savage monks, who represent sham Christianity, merely destroy the body of Hypatia, and have not even attempted to win over her soul. At the time when Philammon first meets Hypatia, her faith in herself and her message is supreme and unshaken. Kingsley's own words, describing the first impression she makes upon the young monk, show the germs of real truth and beauty, which that message contains, in spite of any inconsistencies:

So beautiful! So calm and merciful to him! So enthusiastic towards all which was noble! Had not she too spoken of the unseen world, of the hope of immortality, of the conquest of the spirit over the flesh, just as a Christian might have done? Was the gulf between them so infinite? If so, why had her aspirations awakened echoes in his own heart,—echoes, too, just such as the prayers and lessons of the Laura used to awaken? If the fruit was so like, must not the root be like also?—Could that be a counterfeit? That a minister of Satan in the robes of an angel of light? Light at least it was. purity, simplicity, courage, earnestness, tenderness, flashed out from eye, lip, gesture....

The essence of sham Christianity, which pervaded all parts of the later Empire, and was not confined to the great cities of Rome and Alexandria, is shown by contrast in the description of the impression the monks had made upon the young Philammon:

The men were coarse, fierce, noisy, so different from her! Their talk seemed mere gossip,—scandalous too, and hard judging most of it; about that man's private ambition, and that woman's proud looks; and who had stayed for the Eucharist the Sunday before, and who had gone out after the sermon; and how the majority who did not stay, could possibly dare to go, and how the minority who did not go could possibly dare to stay.... Endless suspicions, sneers, complaints ... what did they care for the eternal glories and the beatific vision? Their one test for all men and things, from the patriarch to the prefect, seemed to be,—did he or it advance the cause of the Church?—which Philammon soon discovered to mean their own cause, their influence, their self-glorification.

Criticism such as this the Church of Rome in Kingsley's day took to itself, and resented. But Kingsley's criticism was directed against sham Christianity, wherever it existed, (not solely against the Church of Rome). Moreover, *Hypatia* is not so much *against* sham Christianity as *for* true Christianity. Let us return to Kingsley's heroine. Hypatia, the beauty of whose thought has been suggested in a preceding paragraph, does not remain resolute to the end. Her attempt to prove that all that is noble and beautiful has its source somewhere in the old pagan system of philosophy, is as fine an attempt as could be made. But she has undertaken the impossible, and her failure is certain. Her pathetic subjection to the hypnotism and magic of old Miriam seems in a way to portend her tragic death. Her weakness at the end makes it appear that the author did not intend determination to be her most striking virtue. Why is it that, even in her martyrdom, Hypatia does not arouse the reader's sympathy as some of the other characters do? It would seem that her position on a pedestal above the ordinary run of mankind deprives her of the sympathy she would otherwise deserve. But is this all? Her aloofness from the multitude, her contempt for the rabble seem almost justified; but are they, in a final analysis of the truth? Recall Kingsley's words, "My idea is to set forth Christianity as the only really democratic creed, and philosophy, above all spiritualism, as the most aristocratic creed." Let us apply the last part of this statement to Hypatia. She denies entirely the salvation of her *aristocratic creed* to the common herd, and to such as Pelagia, the harlot. This is what finally repulses Philammon, in what forms the climax of the story. Moreover, Hypatia as a last resort has been forced to a belief in the "spiritualism", (for such it is), which old Miriam offers, but does not herself accept. This part of the story shows the aristocratic nature of philosophy as a creed, and especially the sham of spiritualism.

And now let us consider the first part of the quotation just made. How does Kingsley set forth the value of true Christianity "as the only really democratic creed"? He starts by portraying the simplicity of life in the Laura and of Philammon's early training. When Philammon reaches Alexandria, he does not scruple to risk his life for an unfortunate negress, and he lives with the little porter on the most democratic terms. Moreover, the generous care of the sick shown in the daily visitations of Cyril, Peter the Reader, and the parabolani, entirely overbalances the inconsistency, or even vindictive cruelty, which they tolerate in the name of the Church. But the most striking evidence of Christianity as a democratic creed, is seen in the character of Raphael Aben-Ezra, the converted Jew. If one is assiduous in seeking parallels, it is possible to see in the early life of Raphael traces of the Byronic hero. But just as Kingsley shows the falsity of "Egyptian magic", which had been made important in earlier novels, so he shows the falsity of any touches of Byronism which the character of Raphael may display. He brings this character out of the mazes of self-conceit and skepticism into something higher and nobler. Raphael, though born to luxury and aristocratic ease, has drained the cup of pleasure to the dregs, and is willing to exchange aristocratic ease for democratic poverty. He has also exhausted the resources of philosophy, and has been thus prepared to appreciate more fully the higher truth of Christianity. If one is to draw an inference from biography, Kingsley has portrayed something of the early doubts of his own mind, in the mental struggles of Raphael. Raphael Aben-Ezra is perhaps as well-done as any character in the novel. His calm reflections on life in general make possible for us a more detached view and a clearer interpretation of the life of the time. The "philosophic" coolness, (to use a word which he himself despised), with which he exchanges the role of prince for that of beggar, gives evidence that he is genuine and sincere. The depths of his character do not really come to light, however, until in Italy he gets the first faint ray of genuine hope, a hope which grows stronger from that time on. He is enabled to consider this hope as legitimate and consistent with the words of God, whether Christian or Hebrew, by the kindly advice of Synesius. But Raphael's real conversion takes place as he listens to the inspiring words of St. Augustine, who is preaching not only *to* but *for* the rough Roman legionaries. What wonder that he was able to win them, heart and soul, when, as Raphael says: "He has been speaking to these wild beasts as to sages and saints; he has been telling them that God is as much with them as with prophets and psalmists.... I wonder if Hypatia with all her beauty, could have touched their hearts as he has done." There is in this passage the whole essence of Christianity as a democratic creed. The conversion of Raphael prepares the way for his intellectual triumph over Hypatia, whom he all but convinces of the truth of his new creed. And the conclusion of the story, portraying the humble Christian self-sacrifice of Philammon, his sister and the other important characters, completes the truthful presentation of Christianity as a democratic creed.

Kingsley's *Hypatia* possesses a depth of insight and a richness of instruction which are equalled in few novels, historical or otherwise. But what Kingsley achieved in *Hypatia* may be summed up, for one who is studying the novel of Roman life, as follows: First, he gave a complete picture of life in the Roman Empire in an accurate historical setting. Secondly, in portraying the climax of the struggle between Christianity and the Roman world, he showed the intimate connection and universal relations, of life in the time of the Roman Empire, with life in the ages which precede and follow it. In the first of these achievements, no novelist has really surpassed Kingsley; in the second, no one has come near equalling him. In regard to the first achievement, Kingsley's faithfulness to history and to the life of the fifth century, it can be said that his "history" has been criticised, for its alleged inaccuracy, by pedants of the malignant school of criticism, for whom history exists only as a means for tripping up their betters. The hollow sham of such criticism is apparent, if we merely allow to Kingsley the freedom accorded to any historical novelist. He has in every respect lived up to the promise of his masterful preface, in which he says: "I have in my sketch of Hypatia and her fate, closely followed authentic history, especially Socrates' account of the closing scenes, as given in *Book* III, *Sec.* 15, of his *Ecclesiastical History*." He also follows authentic history in all other parts of the story where this is essential, adopting the wise method, already discussed, of mingling historical characters and events with imaginary characters and events. When he is not making use of history, he is nevertheless true to the spirit of history. His faithfulness to the life of the times is all that he promises in these words of the *Preface*: "I have labored honestly and industriously to discover the truth, even in its minutest details, and to sketch the age, its manners and its literature as I found them,—altogether artificial, slipshod, effete, resembling far more the times of Louis Quinze than those of Sophocles and Plato." In regard to Kingsley's second achievement in *Hypatia*, it may be said that in portraying "the last struggle between the young Church and the Old World," (*Preface*), he showed the significance of a short period of history, when fitted into the larger scheme of universal history. In the conclusion of *Hypatia*, he says, "I have shown you New Foes under an Old Face—your own likeness in toga and bonnet.... There is nothing new under the sun. The thing which has been, it is that which shall be." Other writers of the novel of Roman life have shown with consummate art the thing which has been,—Christian and Pagan; none have equalled Kingsley in showing that it is also the thing which shall be. And even those who refuse to draw a moral from any piece of fiction, may read with infinite profit and pleasure the great novel which Kingsley's scholarly insight into the life of the Roman Empire enabled him to write.

John Henry Newman was a churchman, who became a bitter opponent of Kingsley; his scholarship was profound, and his early religious training, received from his French Huguenot mother, was along Calvinistic lines. He knew the Bible, it is said, almost by heart. He was led to go over to the Church of Rome by his own studies, since he came to believe that they furnished arguments in support of the Church of Rome, rather than against it. He came to feel with conviction, that the argument that "antiquity was the true exponent of the doctrines of Christianity," really supported the Church of Rome. In this he was directly opposed to Kingsley. It is commonly stated that Newman's novel *Callista*, (1855), was written in answer to Kingsley's *Hypatia*, and this is probably correct. The climax of the public controversy between Kingsley and Newman, however, did not come until 1864, almost ten years later. In his *Postscript* to *Callista*, Newman refers to Lockhart's *Valerius* in such a way as to imply that it is the only other important novel of Roman life, which presents the struggles of Christianity in a philosophical light. He thus intentionally disregards Kingsley's recently published *Hypatia*. *Callista* is the story of a martyr in the African Church, under the Decian persecution. Its scene is laid in Sicca Veneria, near Carthage, and its portrayal of life in the Roman Empire is accurate and realistic. The heartlessness of the Roman magistrates,—both in their persecution of the Christians and in their characteristic strokes of policy in dealing with the mob,—reveals the spirit of Roman life. Local color is especially good, the description of the plague of locusts being the best that exists anywhere in literature, (not excepting even the Bible). Newman follows Kingsley in making his heroine a girl of Greek descent, whose ideas of the beauty which she saw in paganism led her to be repulsed by the religion of the Crucified God. But unlike Hypatia, Callista becomes entirely converted.

The finest piece of writing in Newman's novel, however, is the scene between Callista and Agellius, in which she repudiates Christianity. St. Cyprian, who had been mentioned by Kingsley, is brought into *Callista*; and others high in the Church play a part in the story. Cyprian says the discipline of the Church had become less firm in the interval before the Decian persecution. The author is thus enabled to show that the Church was strengthened by this persecution. To mention familiar elements, magic appears in *Callista*, in the spells and herbs of a witch, which result in her victim being possessed of a demon; the labyrinth motive also appears in the description of the secret passages, by which Callista escapes and which enable the Christians to remain concealed. In any final analysis *Callista* cannot be compared with Kingsley's *Hypatia*. In spite of some very fine passages, it is lacking in uniform excellence. In its portrayal of life in the Roman empire, and in its handling of Christianity it falls short of the deep significance intended. There is indeed too much theological discussion. While *Callista* is a novel of Roman life, and can be read as such, it leans somewhat in the direction of the story of religious instruction, a kind of fiction we have mentioned as an offshoot of the novel of Roman life. Here we may recall that *Fabiola* by Cardinal Wiseman, had appeared the year before *Callista*; *Fabiola* represents the story of religious instruction *par excellence*. Cardinal Wiseman had been for a number of years Professor of Oriental languages at Roman University in Rome, and it is likely that his study of Roman antiquities at Rome would have enabled him to make *Fabiola* a novel of Roman life; instead he made it a stereotyped story of religious instruction. This oft-rewritten horror continues to afford the young the opportunity to enjoy killing off martyrs to their hearts' content. We thus find it necessary again to dismiss the story of religious instruction from primary consideration, but to remember its presence in the background. Stories of this kind, by the prominent place they gave to Christianity, set a precedent which seemed to bind authors of the novel of Roman life to a considerable extent.

After the publication of *Callista*, a number of preachers, who wrote stories of religious instruction, were enabled by their scholarship, to embellish their work to some extent with a portrayal of Roman life. But even so, their work was often intended primarily for younger readers; their books are commonly classed as juvenile. Books of this kind were written by the Rev. John Neale, the Rev. A. D. Crake, the Rev. G. S. Davies and the Rev. A. J. Church. The last-named author was the most scholarly; and his work was excluded in Section I of this study, rather because it was intended for boys than because it represented the story of religious instruction. In considering the work of preachers, we have to pass over some years before we come to the truly great portrayal of life at Rome in the form of fiction, which is seen in Canon Frederic W. Farrar's *Darkness and Dawn*, (1892). This is called by its author *An Historic Tale*, and he distinctly says it is not a novel; but in spite of his modest estimate of his own work, *Darkness and Dawn* is a great novel in every respect, except that it lacks a highly-developed artificial plot. And such a plot is unnecessary, since the element of suspense and even a certain unity of effect are attained merely by a faithful and realistic narration of events, either historical or characteristic of the time. Canon Farrar saw that the age of Nero supplied the best material for the work he contemplated; and in portraying life at Rome in Nero's time with realistic effect, he has surpassed every other English novelist who has written of that period, and is not himself surpassed even by Sienkiewicz, the Polish author of *Quo Vadis*, (1895).

In writing *Darkness and Dawn*, Canon Farrar made full, though judicious, use of his profound scholarship, which in its thoroughness equals that of Charles Kingsley. He equals Kingsley's *Hypatia* in his portrayal of life in the past,— "the thing which has been,"—though he does not attempt in quite the same way to show that it is also "the thing which shall be." In spite of its figurative title, *Darkness and Dawn* does not quite bring the reader to the same realization of the onward sweep of history, the march of civilization, the gradual victory of Christianity, that *Hypatia* does. But in presenting the contrasts in Christian and Pagan life at Rome with faithful exactness, and in terms of the life of today, Farrar teaches his lesson in a different way. While he does not fit his picture of a period of history into the scheme of universal history in the same way that Kingsley does, he portrays the life of the time of Nero with a minuteness of detail which had not been attempted by Kingsley in his portrayal of the life of the Roman Empire in *Hypatia*. Farrar leaves the reader more to derive his own lesson from the facts,—but the sermon is there and may be considered universal in its application. It is only fair, however, to consider *Darkness and Dawn* chiefly for its portrayal of Roman life. As has been hinted, there is a distinct difference in the method of Farrar's portrayal of the past, from that used by Kingsley. Kingsley selects what he considers the important things in the life of the past, and shows their significance. Farrar, on the other hand, gives everything which may be of any consequence, with the most minute exactness of detail. Kingsley's history had been unfairly criticised; Farrar's is beyond criticism. Farrar not only sifts and weighs the finest points in matters of historical accuracy, but also gives the most painstaking and detailed description of manners, customs, habits, dress, and all other things which aid the reader in obtaining an intimate knowledge of the time with which his story deals.

Between the date of publication of *Hypatia*, (1853), and that of *Darkness and Dawn*, (1892), there had come about a marked change in methods of scholarship, especially of classical scholarship; and the effect of this is to be seen in *Darkness and Dawn*. This change in methods of scholarship is chiefly characterized by an insistence upon the minute analysis of historical facts, and of the manners of the ancients. Its effect upon the English novel of Roman life is due to the influence of the painstaking research made by scholars, usually Germans, in the field of Roman private life and Roman archæology; and to the influence of novels of Roman life which made use of such research, and were written by Germans. This influence will be discussed more thoroughly, when we have concluded our study of the English novel of Roman life as written by Churchmen.

The time of Nero's reign at Rome is so crowded with historical events of interest that Farrar was enabled to make nearly all important events in his novel, *Darkness and Dawn*, either absolutely true to history, or so closely connected with history, that they might actually have happened at the time when they are supposed to have happened. The few unimportant and intentional anachronisms he has made are explained candidly in his preface. The events described in the novel, though nearly all of them actually happened in Nero's reign, represent in kind and variety nearly all events which are narrated in other important novels of Roman life. The scenes portrayed are all thoroughly typical of life in ancient Rome. Neither Christian nor pagan life is overemphasized, although a natural and truthful contrast is made of them. Scenes in Nero's palace, in the forum, in the crowded streets of Rome, at the amphitheatre, at the law-courts, and occasionally in the fashionable suburbs of the city, or at Nero's various resorts away from Rome, are portrayed with a fidelity which cannot be questioned. And wherever it is possible to make a scene of realistic effect out of an actual historical event, or to add historical details to a scene which significantly portrays Roman life, the author does so. Yet in spite of the fact that so many scenes in Farrar's novel are taken from history, it is by no means made heavy or overcrowded, with historical detail. Every detail is made significant and interesting, and put in its proper place, so that the general effort is not one of laborious effort but of consummate art. The minutiae of the picture, while effective in themselves, do not obscure its larger lines. Few authors could have presented such a mass of historical detail and intimate information of the life of Rome in a single volume with such fine realistic effect. Farrar was able to make his scholarship count in producing a noble work of fiction; while others in attempting a similar thing were only able to compile what were practically dry hand-books of Roman antiquities.

In its portrayal of character *Darkness and Dawn* is equally true to life and history. So much is known of so many important historical characters of Nero's time, that it becomes not only possible, but even advisable, to make use of only historical characters in a novel which deals with this period. Realizing this, Farrar dispensed almost entirely with imaginary characters. But he selected a large number of historical characters representing all ranks and conditions of life. And since some of these are taken from humble life, and do not play an important part in history, the author found it necessary to describe the course of their lives from his own imagination, aided by his thorough knowledge of the life of the time. It proved, for example, a very happy device to devote a considerable part of the narrative to a description of the wanderings of the runaway slave, Onesimus; for by this means the author was able to bring in many incidents, showing the variety of experiences that even a Roman slave might have. Onesimus is in fear of crucifixion; and is actually sentenced to the recognized punishment for a certain offense, of being thrown into the sea, sewed into a sack with a dog, a cat, and a viper. He also meets the King of the Grove at Aricia, a circumstance which reminds one of perhaps the most "pagan" of pagan customs surviving in the vicinity of Rome, as late as the time of Nero. Only a few of Farrar's characters are unimportant historically, while the mere names of the others remind the reader of history. Agrippina, Nero, Seneca, Burrus, Pomponia, Acte, Poppæa, Tigellinus, St. John, and St. Paul are all important historical figures. Farrar relates with accurate historical detail all the necessary facts concerning them; but he really brings them out of the realm of mere history, and makes them stand before one as real men and women like ourselves.

Where Farrar particularly excels is in his portrayal of the development of character; and in his delineation of the aspect which a conspicuous character will assume in the presence of death or of a great emergency. The portrayal of the development of Agrippina's character is particularly fine, even though death takes her from the scene. She is shown as a character who combines strength of determination with a marked weakness in certain other ways. Her determination is shown in the pursuit of her ambition to gain and hold absolute power. Her weakness is seen to increase from the time when she begins to realize that Nero no longer feels her influence. She finally sinks to abject despair when she becomes certain that the nearness of her death is only a question of time. The changes of Nero's character are also portrayed with masterful strokes. At first he is an ingenuous, sweet-natured boy, guided in the main by the advice of Agrippina and of his tutor, the philosopher Seneca; he only gives, in occasional fits of temper, the vaguest suggestions of what he was to become later. Farrar is careful to show that in passing from the sphere of boyhood to manhood and the duties of imperial office, Nero carried with him a certain puerility,—indeed remained puerile until his death. The author also shows how the germs of the most contemptible qualities of Nero were really fostered by Agrippina, who, while weakly pampering him, little realized how soon he would outgrow her control. Nero's degeneration into the cruel monster and shallow buffoon well known to history is fearlessly painted by Farrar. His contemptible fear of death, and self-pity when death is certain, though suggested by history, are brought home to the reader with a realistic effect surpassing that of any merely historical narrative. Somewhat in contrast to Nero's death is that of Seneca, who was compelled to commit suicide by Nero's decree. Seneca meets death with the resignation of a pagan philosopher, but perhaps not with true heroism. It remains for the Christians, St. Paul and St. John, to enable the author, by a simple narration of their suffering, to portray the unflinching courage and sublime hope of truly great characters in their hours of trial. Neither the stories of these two saints nor that of Nero's living torches, is overdone, however. Nor is undue use of the sensational made in the revelation of the orgies at Nero's revels, and the description of scenes in the arena. The author simply shows Christianity in the lives of a few historical characters such as St. Paul, St. John, Pomponia, Acte and Onesimus; he is not unfair, and is thoroughly accurate, in his portrayal of the pagans. He gives impartially both sides of the picture,—the light and shadow which the title of his novel implies. Its portrayal of human life, Christian and pagan, and its revelation of human character, give *Darkness and Dawn* the right to share with *Hypatia* a position of preeminence among English novels describing life in the Roman Empire, and owing their value in large part to the scholarship of great preachers.

Canon Farrar's other great novel was called *Gathering Clouds* (1895), and has for its scene Constantinople in the days of St. Chrysostom. Besides the fact that the date of its story is rather late, the scene of the novel makes it inadvisable for us to consider it at length; especially since the author's other novel has just furnished ample evidence of his ability to portray life at Rome; and he could gain nothing by transferring the scene to Constantinople. Alexandria, in which much of the scene of Kingsley's *Hypatia* is laid, has been considered as the metropolis of a Roman province. But Constantinople in Chrysostom's time was not in a province of the Western Empire, but was the capital of the Eastern Empire. And, while there are many interesting parallels to life at Rome to be found in novels dealing with Constantinople, as capital of the Eastern Empire, it has seemed best not to consider such novels in detail, in a discussion of the novel of Roman life. In fact, the only other important English novel, which has for its scene Constantinople when

Rome still remained capital of the Western Empire, is Sir Henry Pottinger's *Blue and Green*. This is a realistic story of the riot arising between the two factions, partisans of the rival colors of the chariot-racing companies, but unfortunately is now out of print.

There remains one other novel of Roman life written by a preacher, which deserves especial consideration. This is the Rev. Sabine Baring-Gould's *Domitia*. If one asks why this novel is especially to be considered, the answer is once more to be found in a realization of the author's scholarly attainments. *Domitia* reveals a careful and minute study of Roman history, and especially of Roman private life. It is full of information regarding the life, habits, and dress of Romans in the time of Nero and Domitian. Instead of burdening his pages with footnotes in fine print, the author conceived the idea that such information could be contained in separate paragraphs and inserted bodily into the narrative; and in carrying out this idea he was so successful that the wealth of information conveyed without serious interruption of the narrative, gives *Domitia* its distinguishing characteristic. When a Roman galley is mentioned in the story, the author inserts a paragraph describing such a galley; when a funeral is to take place, he inserts a similar description of a Roman funeral,—and so with other details of Roman private life and custom. History is inserted into the narrative in the same way, but the author wisely refrains from making too great a use of history. The time with which his novel deals includes part of Nero's reign and all of Domitian's; the interval between them is covered briefly. The most dramatic historical episodes narrated are the death of Nero and the death of Domitian, but other scenes taken from history are realistically portrayed. Nero and Domitian are also the most important historical figures, and their characters are well brought out. The heroine of the novel, Domitia, the wife and supposed cousin of the Emperor Domitian, is not very important in formal history; but from a few hints given by history, the author has drawn a character thoroughly human, and such as might have lived at the time. Her mother, representing the frivolous and self-seeking type of Roman matron, is thoroughly characteristic of the time of Domitian. Her father, the soldier who has given his life to his duty to his country, represents by his character the old Roman virtues, which still survived in the hearts of a few men. While Domitia becomes a Christian, her story is not so told as to emphasize Christianity unduly; and in telling it, the author has given us a notable novel of Roman life, sound in its history and its revelation of Roman private life, and presenting a story of human interest.

Baring-Gould also wrote *Perpetua* (1897), a novel which suggests something of Roman life. Its subject reminds one that he edited *The Lives of the Saints* with an erudition which shows his knowledge of Roman life. *Perpetua* is the story of a Christian martyr to the later Roman persecution at Nimes, in the

Roman province of Gaul. The Emperor Caracalla, by whom the edict for this persecution was issued, does not appear in the story, and, of course, the life in the provincial town of Nimes only vaguely suggests life in the capital. But some customs are represented, which had spread from Rome throughout the provinces. Since *Perpetua* was published the year before *Domitia*, it is probable that their author had some things in mind when writing the former, which he did not use until he wrote the latter novel. Nimes was selected for the scene of *Perpetua*, because the author had visited the town and become familiar with its history and archæology. He was thus able to reconstruct accurately the life of its people, as they thronged the festival of the local divinity, or crowded into the amphitheatre to witness persecution of the Christians. Roman paganism is seen to be losing its grip, since the pagan citizens do not all take the local god very seriously. The element of "magic" in pagan superstition is seen in the deception practiced by the priestesses of the god; they make his voice sound over the town by shouting into a trumpet-shaped amplifier, which magnifies the sound. Another familiar element in the novel of Roman life is seen in the labyrinth motive, which appears when the hero of the story makes his escape from the prison through a dark, vile, and tortuous drain. Christianity, while it appears to be still weak, if one looks upon some of the wavering converts who are represented, is seen to be growing in strength, when one realizes the unyielding faith of Perpetua, and of a few others. But too much is not made of Christianity, and Baring-Gould's novel is not to be considered a story of religious instruction. *Perpetua* is chiefly important to our subject in that it suggests the work which its author was to do in his other novel, *Domitia*. There is little use made in *Perpetua* of important historical events or characters. The heroine's name, "Perpetua," was suggested by that of a martyr of the persecution at Carthage, whose story is well known, and does not belong to the history of Nimes. Since the publication of *Domitia*, no very important novel of Roman life has been written in English by any great scholarly preacher. Many other preachers have written books of considerable merit, which portray something of Roman life; but further discussion of these books is withheld, since they are primarily stories of religious instruction, or are intended only for younger readers.

B. THOROUGHNESS IN SCHOLARSHIP, RESULTING IN PART FROM THE INFLUENCE OF SUCH GERMAN SCHOLARS AS BECKER,—BECKER'S "GALLUS"

We have made some mention of the scholarship of German writers; the Germans were not the only classical scholars whose influence is important in our study, but in some cases made an exceedingly thorough study of the private life of the Romans, and the effect of this is seen upon the English novel of Roman life. An exceedingly careful attention to minute details in the study of the private life of the Romans is seen in the work of Professor W. A. Becker in *Gallus, or Roman Scenes in the Time of Augustus*, published in Leipsic (1838). This is not a novel at all, though it contains some connected material in the form of fiction. The importance of Becker's *Gallus* in its effect upon the novel of Roman life, has been overemphasized by pedantic schoolmen; but it served to show English scholars the necessity for absolute exactness, even to the most minute details, in all matters pertaining to the study of the private life of the Romans. Becker is not in any sense to be considered a pupil of Scott, though his work was published shortly after the world had read the last of Scott's novels. But Becker showed later German followers of Scott how it was possible to present with minute accuracy the life of the Romans; and these German historical novelists who thus portrayed Roman life, had an important influence upon the English novel of Roman life, as has been suggested in connection with Canon Farrar's *Darkness and Dawn*. In *Gallus*, which we have said is not a novel, Becker says (in the Preface), "His original intention was to produce a systematic handbook, but finding this would lead to too much brevity and curtailment, and exclude altogether several minor traits, ... which were highly necessary to a complete portrait of Roman life, he was induced to imitate the example of Bottiger and Mazois, and produce a continuous story, with explanatory notes on each chapter. Those topics which required more elaborate investigation, have been handled at length in Excursus." The "continuous story" which Becker chose was that of "Cornelius Gallus, a man whose fortunate rise from obscurity to splendor and honor, love of Lycoris, and poetical talents, render him not a little remarkable." The author tells the story of Gallus, wherever possible, absolutely in accordance with history. He cites as his sources for this personal history Dio Cassius, Strabo, Suetonius, Vergil, Propertius and Ovid. He says further that "the Augustan age is decidedly the happiest time to select," for a portraiture of Roman manners, since for the study of Roman private life of that period there is abundant source-material. He says that "apart from the numerous antique monuments which have been dug up, and placed in museums, our most important authorities on Roman private life are the later poets, as Juvenal, Martial, Statius: then Petronius, Seneca, Suetonius, the two Plinys, Cicero's speeches and letters, the elegiac poets, and especially Horace. Next come the grammarians and the digests; while the Greek authors, as Dionysius of Halicarnassus, Plutarch, Dio Cassius, Lucian, Athenaeus, and the lexicographers, as Pollux, still further enlighten us." In his careful citation of sources, and careful choice of what were the best sources, Becker pointed the way for all those who wrote of Roman life, whether they wrote in the form of the novel or not. He succeeded in making his work what he wished it to be, "a desirable repository of whatever is most worth knowing about the private life of the Romans." Moreover, while Becker's work does not pretend to be a novel, and is far too learned and ponderous to be called a novel, he unconsciously aided later writers of the novel of Roman life by showing them what a mistake it would be to overcrowd such a novel with details of Roman private life. At the same time they might derive some profit from *Gallus* as a model of accuracy in such matters. Becker's work was a step in the proof of the fact that the later novel of Roman life must be accurate and precise in matters of scholarship. It is true that Bulwer had done somewhat the same thing that Becker claims to do in *Gallus*, but Becker's meticulous regard for detail, while showing English novelists what to avoid, also aided them to a more full appreciation of the necessity for absolute accuracy, even in matters of small importance.

C. GERMAN FOLLOWERS OF SCOTT—THE GERMAN NOVEL OF ROMAN LIFE; ITS INFLUENCE ON THE ENGLISH NOVEL

If Becker and other German scholars showed scholars elsewhere the necessity of thoroughness in classical scholarship, and added much to their study of Roman life, it is equally true that Sir Walter Scott showed the world the possibilities of the historical novel. Needless to say Scott had imitators throughout Europe and America; and not only was his success immediate, but his influence on the historical novel was a permanent thing. Many who eagerly devoured his novels in boyhood became his imitators in later life. Not a few of these historical novelists were Germans, and some of their finest works deal with the life of ancient Rome. The authors of these novels endeavored to imitate Scott in many of the things which made his historical novels successful; for example, they saw that the life of Rome supplied them with gorgeous historical scenes, just as the life of mediæval times had supplied such scenes to Scott. But they especially resolved to follow Scott in presenting realistic descriptions of manners, and it must be admitted that some of them described the manners of Roman times quite as well as Scott had described the manners of mediæval times. These German novelists, such as George Ebers, were well fitted to describe the manners of Rome, since they were thorough students of Roman things; and they had been shown how these things could be presented, by Becker and other scholars, who wrote some years before them.

In 1876 was published *A Struggle for Rome*, by Julius Sophus Felix Dahn. This is Dahn's greatest novel, and portrays with fine realistic effect the struggle between the Ostrogoths and Belisarius. In this, and in its handling of the character of Totila, it suggests the great novel of George Gissing, *Veranilda* (1904). Another prominent character besides Totila, in Dahn's novel, is Cassiodorus. The scene in part is laid at Ravenna, and the decay and final collapse of the Gothic kingdom are well illustrated. In 1882 Dahn began a series of short novels, illustrating, he says, the spread of Roman civilization, which went hand in hand with the decline of Roman power over the migrating German tribes. The first of these novels is *Felicitas* (1882), which describes the capture of the distinctly Roman town of Claudium Juvavum (now Salzburg), by the Germans. The author gained his material when he was employed at Salzburg, in the archives, library, and museum of Roman antiquities. He added to his fund of thorough information by explorations in the vicinity of the town, finding many Roman things of interest. *Felicitas* well illustrates the thoroughness of research and the acute scientific spirit, which the Germans in a measure gave to the novel of Roman life. It also tells a story of deep human interest. In 1894 Dahn published *A Captive of the Roman Eagles*, a novel which tells the story of Bissula, and portrays the struggle between the Romans and the Alemanni near Lake Constance. This novel is also a model of thoroughness and historical accuracy. Dahn's last novel, which appeared shortly after, was call *The Scarlet Banner* (1864), and paints with a like accuracy the overthrow of the Vandal king, Gelimer, by Belisarius.

The historical novels of George Ebers, and the profound classical scholarship he displayed in some of them, are well known everywhere. While his important series of historical novels, starting with *An Egyptian Princess* (1879), is designed principally to follow the course of history in Egypt, some of its numbers illustrate Roman life and Roman history. In 1881 appeared *The Emperor*, which presents a fine picture of life in the time of Hadrian. While the scene is laid mainly in Egypt, life in Alexandria is shown as presenting a close parallel to that of Rome. The sternness of Roman dominion in Egypt and the growth of Christianity in the Empire are brought home to the reader with many minute touches which show the author's acuteness. The richly pictorial style is well suited to the description of splendid scenes, and the manners of private life are portrayed with accuracy of detail. Ebers also excels in his analysis of character. The Emperor Hadrian, who appears first as a benevolent philosopher, soon shows that he is capable of becoming a cruel tyrant. The character of Hadrian's wife Sabina is also carefully analyzed, while his favorite, the beautiful youth Antinous, plays a prominent part in the story. It is likely that this gave a suggestion to Professor Hausroth (pseud. George Taylor), who made Antinous the hero of his novel of that name, which appeared in the same year as *The Emperor*.

In 1885 Ebers published *Serapis*, which portrays life in Alexandria in the time of Theodosius, and reveals much of Roman customs. The struggle between Christians and pagans is represented as culminating in the destruction of the temple of Serapis, and the demolition of the gigantic image of the god. This was a result of the edict abolishing the worship of idols. The dramatic scene in which the temple of Serapis is defended by a multitude of pagans, who have stored arms there, has appeared many years later in the novel of Roman life of the American author, T. Everett Harré, called *Behold the Woman* (1916). Another interesting point is that *Serapis* contains a splendid scene describing a chariot race, in which a Christian defeats a pagan, after the occurrence of a fatal accident. This scene may have been suggested to Ebers by the famous scene in *Ben Hur* (1880); while on the other hand it is likely that General Wallace, the American author of *Ben Hur*, owes some of his exactness in matters of scholarship to the example of such German scholars as George Ebers.

Another of Ebers' novels which portrayed much of Roman life was *Per Aspera (A Thorny Path)* (1892). While the scene is again Alexandria, *Per Aspera*, like *The Emperor*, shows that city at the time of the visit paid to it by the Roman Emperor. In *Per Aspera* the Emperor is Bassianus, whose nickname, "Caracalla," was derived from his custom of wearing a hood (caracalla). The portrait of Caracalla is well done, showing his physical and mental suffering, his pride, his dreams and his increasing insanity. The Christians are portrayed in a natural light, while pagan customs are well explained, and the splendor, display and wealth of Alexandria dazzle the imagination. The labyrinth motive appears in the mystery of the secret passages of the temple of Serapis. Scenes representing gladiators in the arena are characteristically Roman, while the slaughter of the youths in the parade-ground shows the cruelty of Rome and the power of her Emperor. Yet Ebers, with his usual insight into human character, shows that the Emperor, who could cruelly punish those who had wittily derided him, found his power of little ultimate value to him. In speaking of the Emperor's poor health, mention is made of the great Roman physician, Galen, who plays an important part in Mr. E. L. White's *Andivius Hedulio* (1921).

The next of Ebers' novels to be considered is *Cleopatra* (1894). While it contains many characteristic touches, which show Ebers' knowledge of life in what was soon to become permanently a Roman province, *Cleopatra* is not so much a portrayal of Roman life as a sympathetic interpretation of the later history of Egypt's great queen. Ebers, as usual, is absolutely true to history, but endeavors to present Cleopatra as a human being, subject to strong emotions, rather than as an historical figure. Even Antony appears not so much in the character of a Roman general, as in that of a strong man who influences the character of Cleopatra. The chief value of Ebers' *Cleopatra* lies in the fact that Ebers has come much nearer to presenting the real character of Cleopatra than has any other novelist. Sir Rider Haggard's *Cleopatra* has been mentioned as a poor piece of work, while in Mr. W. S. Davis's excellent novel, *A Friend of Caesar* (1900), Cleopatra is merely represented as a young girl.

A beautiful little novel which Ebers calls *A Question; the Idyll of a Picture by His Friend Alma Tadema* (1881), is written in a style quite different from that of his other novels. Its scene is Sicily, near Aetna, at a "time when the entire earth and air were peopled with gods, nymphs and satyrs."[25] It is mentioned here because in its scene, its theme, and the simplicity and beauty of its style, there is a strong suggestion of the recently published novel of Mr. Eden Phillpotts, *Evander* (1919), the scene of which is prehistoric Italy. *Evander* gives one an idea of the first faint beginnings of Roman life in a semi-mythological setting similar to that of *A Question*.

The novels of Ernst Eckstein were almost as widely read in England and America as those of Ebers. Some of them equal or even surpass Ebers' best work. *Quintus Claudius* (1881), gives a splendid portrayal of life in Rome under Domitian. The author has presented in a single story practically the whole life of Rome, and has described the most noted characters of the time. "The life and manners of all classes at this period were never painted with a bolder pencil than by Eckstein in this masterly romance, which displays as much scholarship as invention."[26] In this review a better expression than "invention" would be "a gifted imagination and a deep insight into human nature." In *Quintus Claudius*, the character of Domitia is interpreted in an entirely different way from that in which Baring-Gould interpreted it in *Domitia* (1898); but this does not mean that either author was untrue to history, since little is known of her, save that she and her Emperor-husband were at variance. In Eckstein's novel the intrigues of Domitia really furnish the central theme, rather than the affairs of the imaginary Quintus Claudius, who spurns her and loves Cornelia. Quintus and Cornelia are very finely characterized, the former being by no means perfect, and subject to the vices of the time, although he later becomes a Christian. Among historical characters the poet Martial is portrayed as the court parasite that he was. The conspiracy against Domitian is described with historical accuracy and fine realistic effect. The book ends with the murder of Domitian and the accession of Trajan. Nerva is mentioned but not as an emperor.

In *Prusias* (1882), Eckstein rises to the greatness of his theme. The story is that of the revolt, in which Roman slaves, under the leadership of Spartacus, rose against Roman oppression. The character of Spartacus, in every respect true to history, is made to represent democracy and freedom. Coming, as it did, shortly after the Civil War had settled the slavery question in America, *Prusias* had a wide reading here. To supplement the fine character of Spartacus, Prusias, the technical hero of the story, is also represented as magnanimous and farsighted, well-fitted to aid the great general of the slaves in inspiring them to fight for freedom. By a stroke of genius, Prusias, who first appears in the disguise of a Chaldean magician, is conceived to be the brother and agent of Mithradates, King of Pontus. Rome's two most powerful enemies are thus allied against her. While Prusias does much of the planning of the conspiracy, he does not overshadow the general of the slaves.

The truly great historical character, Spartacus, is presented with a power not since equaled in fiction, and only approached by the Rev. A. J. Church in his excellent book for boys, *Two Thousand Years Ago* (1885), written shortly afterward. *Prusias* also portrays life in the city of Rome under the republic with accurate detail.

In *The Chaldean Magician* (1886), Eckstein portrays life at Rome under Diocletian. The varied phases of the many-sided life at Rome are brought into the picture in many ways, and Diocletian's persecution of the Christians is given its due place. But as the title implies, the author gives especial attention to the magic arts which were practiced by Chaldean astrologers at Rome. The character of the "Chaldean Magician" had been in Eckstein's mind when he was writing *Prusias*, and he took the opportunity of giving it greater prominence in his novel named for such a character. In fact, from the date of this novel, the figure of the Chaldean astrologer supplants that of the priest who deals in "Egyptian magic," in those novels which deal with magic imported from foreign lands to Rome. It became the fashion for wealthy Romans to keep a Chaldean astrologer in their household, and such a character appears in Baring-Gould's *Domitia*, and in Mr. W. S. Davis's *A Friend of Caesar*.

Eckstein's greatest novel of Roman life was *Nero* (1889). It was impossible for him to surpass the portrayal of the general life of Rome, which he had already made in his earlier novels; but in dealing with life in the time of Nero, he found the greatest opportunity to display his talents. In his faithfulness to the life and history of the time he prepared the way for the two other authors who have written great novels dealing with Nero's time,—Canon Farrar in *Darkness and Dawn* (1892), and H. Sienkiewicz in *Quo Vadis* (1895). He was also closely followed by Hugh Westbury in *Acte* (1890), and by two writers of books for boys, the Rev. A. J. Church in *The Burning of Rome* (1892), and G. A. Henty in *Beric, the Briton* (1892). Eckstein's keenness in portraying the court intrigues of Agrippina, Seneca, and Tigellinus, shows his understanding of human nature. But his greatest triumph is in the analysis of the character of Nero. The early boyhood of Nero, and his ingenuous love for Acte, who is kidnapped and kept hidden by the agents of Agrippina, are revealed with genuine sympathy. And Nero's later development is traced step by step, with a fairness that makes him appear the victim not only of his own weakness, but of circumstance. In his revelation of character, as shown in his handling of the character of Nero or of Spartacus, Eckstein surpasses even the notable work of George Ebers.

REVIEW OF THE INFLUENCE OF GERMAN SCHOLARS AND AUTHORS

It is not intended to overemphasize the importance of the influence of German scholars and authors upon the English novel of Roman life. The influence of work such as that of Becker upon the English novel of Roman life may be described as follows: (1) It stimulated many English scholars to study the life of ancient Rome with a similar insistence upon accuracy in regard to the most minute details of history and archæology; in one or two instances an attempted imitation of work like Becker's is seen in the work of pedantic authors of the novel of Roman life. (2) It served as one of the influences, which led popular writers of the novel of Roman life to realize the need for at least some accurate study of the history and life of Rome. The influence of German novelists such as Ebers and Eckstein, upon the English novel of Roman life, is seen in the more thorough scholarship which such English novels display,—especially after the publication of Eckstein's *Nero*, which is the first of a series of important novels portraying life in Nero's time. This series, as has been said, includes not only Farrar's great novel, *Darkness and Dawn*, and other English fictions, but also the fine work of the Polish author, Sienkiewicz, in *Quo Vadis* (1895). In speaking of the thoroughness of German scholars, it might be said that in some instances German novelists such as Ebers, seem occasionally to have made the mistake of assuming that a mass of particulars heaped together can be shaped into the aspect of a general truth. In pursuing the details of a picture of Roman life, they have lost sight of its larger lines sometimes; but, on the whole, very rarely. We must not forget that there were English scholars, who played their part in impressing upon historical novelists the necessity for accuracy. But the German authors of novels of Roman life, produced so many good novels of this kind in so short a time, that their influence is seen in the work of English novelists, both in regard to the subjects which English writers have chosen, and in the methods of presenting such subjects taken from Roman life.

D. TWO PEDANTIC NOVELS OF ROMAN LIFE

Few novelists have made the mistake of attempting to include in a novel such work as appears in Becker's *Gallus*. But in one or two instances, novelists have tried to crowd their pages with antiquarian knowledge, putting into their narratives matters which Becker would have placed in his Excursus. This pedantic display of knowledge is in itself a defect, and we shall consider separately two novelists who proved to be guilty of it. Miles Gerald Keon, British Colonial Secretary to Bermuda, wrote, in 1866, a novel called *Dion and the Sibyls*. This was published in London. In spite of its pedanticism, it contains some interesting similarities to the much greater work of General Lew Wallace in *Ben Hur* (1880). Like *Ben Hur* it deals with the time of Christ, and a further similarity is seen in the fact that the author does not make the mistake of portraying Christ as one of the central figures, and does not lay much of the scene in Jerusalem. Keon's hero, Dion, also, like Ben Hur, is not too closely identified with Christianity, though he is invited to expound its doctrines before the Emperor. Scenes in Judea in *Dion and the Sibyls* include the banquet at which John the Baptist is beheaded, and a pedantic display of knowledge is made in repeating things told of Herod Agrippa, Herodias, Berenice, and the high priest Caiphas. This display of pedantic knowledge is further seen in the part of the narrative which tells of Dion's meeting with Dionysius the Areopagite, who becomes St. Denis, and brings Christianity to Gaul. But most of the scene of Keon's novel is laid in Rome, and in this part of the story the characters of Tiberius, his brutal eunuch Lygdus, and the wily Sejanus, are portrayed in such a way as to show the author's indefatigable search for details. The only really good scene in the novel is that in which the young Paulus, of the Æmelian family, subdues the famous "Sejan horse" in the amphitheatre. The story of this vicious horse became a tradition, so that Mr. E. L. White would have done well to give the name "Sejanus" to a similar animal in *Andivius Hedulio* (1921), a novel of the time of Commodus; (instead he turns the name into Selinus). In Keon's novel Paulus was directed how to overcome the horse by the sibyl of Cumæ, and as the title suggests, the magic spells of such witches appear prominently in the story; the use of a "love-philtre" suggests *The Last Days of Pompeii* (1834). The mention of a famous acrostic, whose initial letters spell the Greek word for fish, remind one of the use made of this symbol of the early Christians, which appears in later novels of Roman life, notably in *Darkness and Dawn* (1892), and *Quo Vadis*. But *Dion and the Sibyls* is mentioned at this point as an example of pedanticism in the novel of Roman life.

Another example of pedanticism in the novel of Roman life is seen in *The Money God; or The Empire and the Papacy* (1873). It is needless to mention the various matters of detail which the author, M. A. Quinton, mentions in order to display his pedantic knowledge; but it is sufficient to say that he is very learned indeed, and has read extensively in the works of the Latin authors.[27] In some instances he is very inaccurate in the deductions which he makes from his reading, and there are some notable mistakes in topography. The one redeeming feature of the novel is its remarkable handling of a chariot-race scene; the details of this scene are so similar to the details of a scene in *Ben Hur* (1880), that it seems possible that Lew Wallace may have known of Quinton's work. While the scene of the *Money God* is partly laid in Rome, it does not portray Roman life, but rather presents certain details of Roman life in an arbitrary manner, and in confused order. A Roman marriage ceremony is described, and the methods of Roman money-lenders are explained in this arbitrary way. Quinton also wrote *Aurelia: or the Jews of Capena Gate*, a few years before *The Money God*, but I have been unable to obtain this book. In

Dion and the Sibyls, and in *The Money God* we have two very pedantic novels, which, nevertheless, mention some of the things which are mentioned in *Ben Hur*. But before considering *Ben Hur* itself, let us retrace our steps to the year 1843, and from that time follow the course of the popular melodramatic novel of Roman life. This kind of novel represents the class in which *Ben Hur* more properly belongs.

E. NOVELS WRITTEN BY SO-CALLED "POPULAR" NOVELISTS, WHO RELY ON THE MELODRAMATIC FOR THEIR APPEAL; THE DEVELOPMENT OF THE "POPULAR" NOVEL OF ROMAN LIFE FROM 1843 TO THE PRESENT DAY

As has been said, the growing insistence upon thoroughness of scholarship, which is seen in the work of both German and English scholars, resulted not only in a somewhat direct imitation of the methods which appear in Becker's *Gallus* (1838), by a few pedantic novelists; but more especially in an attempted exhibition of scholarship by "popular" novelists, who wrote novels of Roman life after this date. These "popular" novelists were men who either turned out novels by the score, or produced a few novels of the made-to-order variety; who sought for material with the idea of obtaining "grist for the mill," rather than of writing a masterpiece. Such novelists have in most cases relied for their appeal upon the use of melodramatic material; but even these "popular" novelists soon came to realize the necessity of sound scholarship to any author who intends to attempt a novel of Roman life. In the class of "popular" novelists, we shall also include those novelists whose principal desire seems to have been to tell a "rattling good story" or to present a series of gorgeous pictures from the life of the past,—though in some cases a more serious purpose seems to underlie work of this description. We shall begin our review of the "popular," melodramatic novel of Roman life with the novel of Ellen Pickering, which appeared in 1843; but the "gorgeous romance," which is a direct development of the "popular" novel, did not reach its height until considerably later. After 1843 all true novels of Roman life make at least some pretense of thorough scholarship.

Ellen Pickering, an American authoress, who turned out a score of "popular" novels, wrote as one of the last of them, *Julia of Baiae; or the Days of Nero* (1843). She clearly shows her realization both of the necessity for thorough scholarship in matters of history, and of her own shortcomings in such matters. This is plain from the diffidence of her preface to the novel, and from the fact that it was published anonymously. The story of the death of Burrus, and the appearance of Vespasian in the Praetorian guards, are matters introduced not in strictly historical order. But otherwise the book has no great faults. It is, however, not even intended as a great novel, and is only cited here in illustration of the fact that a reasonable display of scholarship was coming to be demanded even of popular novelists. *Julia of Baiae* appeared two years after the last of the Rev. Ware's novels (*Julian*, 1841), and was dedicated to the Rev. Fred. J. Goodwin, M. A., Rector of St. George's Church, Flushing, N. Y. Yet, while it contains a story of the martyrs, it is not to be considered a story of religious instruction, but as an attempt at a popular novel with a rather feeble essay at classical scholarship.

Wilkie Collins, who wrote *Antonina* in 1850, is a curious example of a novelist possessed of rather high talents, yet turning out novels which were made to the order of the popular taste, and did not have the stamp of permanence. Collins belongs to the school of Dickens rather than that of Scott; and he develops the melodramatic side of Dickens, while dispensing with Dickens' humor. In fact, in *Antonina*, Collins goes back somewhat toward the style of the Gothic romancers, who preceded Scott. Bleak mountainsides, dark caverns and rushing torrents suggest the "Gothic" terror. The labyrinth motive appears as one of the principal motives of the story, in that its chief character, a priest of Serapis, spends his life in digging a secret passage through the walls of Rome, that he may thwart the Christians by letting in the pagan invaders. This motive is also used in a description of the secret passages under the temple of Serapis. Another "Gothic" element is shown in the ghastly scene at the banquet where guests and host resolve to die before leaving their couches. While the story describes the siege and sack of Rome by the Goths in 410 A. D., the invaders are made to appear less like the real Goths than like the characters of the "Gothic" romancers. In fact, the few historical characters of *Antonina* are not very well done, and its history is not very good. But in writing this, his first novel, Collins realized that he must be fairly accurate in matters of history,—and in his descriptions of Roman life in *Antonina* he sometimes achieves fine realistic effect.

It would be unfair to brand the excellent work of Henry W. Herbert as that of a "popular novelist," since he displays a profound scholarship not usually found in the "popular novelist." But it may be fair to consider that one of his aims was to tell a "rattling good story," and in this he was certainly successful. His one important novel was called *The Roman Traitor; or Days of Cicero, Cato, and Catiline*, and was published in Philadelphia in 1853. It is a powerful story of the conspiracy of Catiline against the Roman republic in 63 B. C. The character of Catiline is portrayed with masterful strokes, while those of Lentulus, Cethegus, and other conspirators, are also well-done. Cicero, Cato, and the young Julius Caesar, also appear in a natural light, though of these three, only Cicero is made to play an important part. Scenes in the Senate and in the houses of the nobility are life-like, yet not over-done. The author has succeeded admirably in portraying real men and women, their thoughts, desires and passions. Scenes of politics, luxury, and intrigue, ring true to life. Speeches assigned to Cicero, Caesar, and Cato, are literal translations from the works of Cicero and Sallust. Yet the author makes them seem as real as though the words were being spoken today. He also shows a thorough knowledge of the topography of ancient Rome. Certain "Gothic" elements appear in the story, especially near the end, where the scene is a dark, dismal recess, overlooking a fearful chasm. But the general style surpasses that of any Gothic romance and is suggestive of Scott. Fine as it is in its portrayal of Roman life, *The Roman Traitor* is even finer in its telling of a remarkable story. It is also the only really effective handling of the conspiracy of Catiline in the form of fiction.

The chief aim of Major G. J. Whyte-Melville in *The Gladiators* (1863), is obviously to present a "gorgeous romance," replete with hair-raising episodes. Whyte-Melville, who is the first of the brilliantly sensational writers of the "gorgeous romance" of Roman life in English, is well known for his novels of sporting life in England. In *The Gladiators* he portrays the brilliant and corrupt society of ancient Rome in the first century, A. D., in a way which suggests his knowledge of a similar brilliant sporting society in modern England. In his use of history in *The Gladiators*, Whyte-Melville is fairly accurate. While not a man of profound scholarship, he fortunately found his historical material in a compact and readily accessible form, in the work of the Jewish historian Josephus. There is not much genuine history in the first part of *The Gladiators*, in which portion the scene is laid in Rome; but in the latter part of the novel, the author followed Josephus, in his wish to find plenty of exciting and romantic episodes. It is interesting to note, for example, that the story of the secret passage through the walls of Jerusalem (which illustrates the labyrinth motive), was taken by Whyte-Melville from Josephus. Many other instances could be cited of Whyte-Melville's indebtedness to Josephus. Croly, it will be recalled, followed Josephus to some extent, but made a more scholarly and imaginative use of his material. The latter part of *The Gladiators*, in which the author relies more on the guidance of history, is better than the first part of the story, and contains some really fine descriptions of episodes in the siege of Jerusalem. However, that part of the story which deals with life at Rome and the defeat of Vitellius is accurate in its portrayal of some characteristic scenes of Roman times. In general, *The Gladiators*, while it has an impossible plot, and consists mainly of a series of gorgeous scenes, may be said to portray Roman life very well in most of its scenes. It lacks unity in its story and probability in some of its details, and this is what prevents its having a completeness of realistic effect.

It would be absurd as well as unfair to call *Ben Hur* (1880), Gen. Lew Wallace's great novel of Roman life, "merely a popular" novel. A gorgeous romance it certainly is,—but this is not all. *Ben Hur* has been and still is "popular" in the best sense of the word. Some of the finest novels of Roman life, even such great works as Kingsley's *Hypatia* and Canon Farrar's *Darkness and Dawn*, make their strongest appeal to the cultured few; *Ben Hur* appeals with equal power to all. Moreover, some novels of Roman life interest every one for a time, yet later lose their power to interest; *Ben Hur* has become a permanent thing, appealing to the popular taste of all time. *Ben Hur* is the first novel of Roman life in English which has with uniform success combined a high seriousness and sincerity of tone, with a use of the sensational achieving the utmost in realistic effect. Such a combination was only partly attempted in *Hypatia*,—which only makes a limited use of the sensational,—and was only equalled in isolated parts of *Salathiel*. *Ben Hur* has been called a romance, but as one reads it, his feeling is not, "This is romance," but "This is life!"

Ben Hur is so universally known, that it is needless to review it here. It has never ceased to be sold in English-speaking countries; while it has been translated into French, German, Bohemian, Swedish, Turkish, Spanish, Portuguese and Arabic, and printed in raised letters for the blind. Its dramatization has also increased its popularity. Hence we need now only consider a few points about *Ben Hur* in regard to its relation to our subject. In the first place, *Ben Hur* is definitely a novel of Roman life, though its scene only goes to the city of Rome in occasional brief explanatory paragraphs. Other novels of Roman life so far considered have deserved to be called such, either because their scene was laid (at least in part) in Rome, or because it was laid chiefly in some great city of the Empire, (as Alexandria in *Hypatia*), in which life very strongly resembled the life of Rome. But from *Ben Hur*, more than from any other novel, one gets a sense of other related parts of the Roman world. Other novelists, as Croly in *Salathiel*, have successfully carried their characters to different parts of the Roman world, and have described scenes, which were of deep significance, but which none the less were associated in one's mind with a definitely limited place. But in *Ben Hur* from the beginning of the story, when the three "wise men," representing the antiquity of Egypt, the learning of the East, and the culture of Greece, meet and pursue the common purpose of their lives, one perceives that the important events and even minor episodes of the story are to be of such tremendous significance, that they throw off the limitations of time and place. The events of *Ben Hur* are accurately assigned by the author to different historical places, but they really belong not so much to separate, individual parts of the Roman world, as to the whole of that world. Christ was born in Palestine (the scene of most of *Ben Hur*), but His message was to the whole world,—and the world was then Roman. Ben Hur was a Jew, but the message he received was for Jew and Gentile, Roman master and Roman slave. That the entire world was Roman in the time of Christ is shown by Wallace with great care and fidelity. Wherever the story takes one, he meets with characteristic Roman scenes. Scenes in Palestine show the unmistakable marks of the Roman oppressor, and the bitter hatred with which Rome's power is regarded. We meet with Roman soldiers, a Roman slave-gang, we witness the departure of a Roman galley, and a Roman fight at sea; we behold the conclusion of a Roman all-night revel, while the Romans take precedence over all other celebrants in the Grove of Daphne. Even the chariot-race scene,[28] the most famous in *Ben Hur*, could have been transferred to Rome, and is characteristic of the Roman world.

How then does *Ben Hur* show the coming of Christ into the world, the material part of which was under Roman sway? The novel is called in its alternative title *A Tale of the Christ*,—and such it is. The figure of Christ appears when he is a babe worshipped by the Magi, and later in scenes near the time of the Crucifixion; but these scenes are based on Scripture rather than created by Wallace. We have spoken of the fact that no novel of Roman life can be successful, if it makes Christ the central figure or character. *Ben Hur* does not do so; but its author shows enough of the life and death of the lowly Nazarene to convince one of His Divine Influence upon the Roman world, which has become the world of today. Ben Hur as he listened to the preaching of Jesus, and gazed upon His wonderful countenance, remembered having seen Him before. "That the look so calm, so pitiful, so loving, had somewhere in the past beamed upon him as that moment it was beaming on Balthazar, became an assurance. Faintly at first, at last a clear light, a burst of sunshine, the scene by the well at Nazareth what time the Roman guard was dragging him to the galleys returned, and all his being thrilled." This quotation is typical of the story of *Ben Hur; a Tale of the Christ*. The mother and sister of Ben Hur suffered misfortune at the hands of the Romans, and were only freed from the cruelty of the Roman world by their acceptance of and meeting with The Master. Lew Wallace is equally great in his portrayal of the material life of Rome and the spiritual life of Christ.

Having chosen his subject, Wallace wisely refrained from making any very great use of Roman history, or of Roman historical characters not important in the Bible story. But just as the scenes of his novel are typical of life in the Roman world, so his characters exhibit the variety of race, creed and nationality to be found in the people Rome ruled. Beside a number of different types of Hebrew character which the author portrays, there are at least two kinds of Romans in *Ben Hur*, the proud, cruel oppressor, in Messala, and the magnanimous benefactor, in Quintus Arrius. Other characters represent the sage of whatever nationality, the youthful Greek with his perfect physical beauty, the Arab sheik, the seductive siren of the Nile, the devout Christian, and the pagan priestess. But Wallace does not rely too much on atmosphere or local color. His knowledge of Roman history was sound. While Messala, an imaginary character, is important in the story, Sejanus, who controlled the politics of Rome, is given his proper place in the background. In fact, the scholarship of Wallace was sound in every way. While he did not finish his schooling according to the prescribed course, he completed his own education more thoroughly than most men do. He was a great reader of good books, and at the age of 19, had read every book in his father's library,—700 standard works. He continued to be a great reader and student, and formed a large library of his own. Besides his reading Wallace had a rich experience of life on the battlefield and in public life, and was peculiarly well fitted to understand with sympathy all sorts and conditions of men. *Ben Hur* is the only other novel of Roman life, besides *Salathiel*, to arouse successfully the reader's sympathy for a Jewish hero. In his presentation of Ben Hur as a slave, Wallace showed his realization of antiquity of the slavery question; and he had shortly before done his part in settling forever that question. His sympathetic understanding of men, women, and little children of the present aided him in portraying with sympathy various types of character seen in the life of the past. *Ben Hur* is a novel which voices the hopes and aspirations of the common people of all the world.

Any estimate of the absolute value of Ben Hur must place Lew Wallace's novel very high indeed. If one discounts the great influence the book has had upon its many readers, and considers it simply as a piece of art, it still ranks very high. While *Ben Hur* is said to have brought its author more sudden fame than any other novel has brought to an American author, this fame which came suddenly, did not as suddenly depart. If he is judged by the merits of *Ben Hur*, Wallace deserves to be ranked, as a novelist, with other great American novelists, such as Cooper, Hawthorne and Howells. In the opinion of a noted authority on American literature, *Ben Hur* "is in every respect a great novel."[29] And it is impossible to differ with this opinion. Reduced to its lowest terms, all adverse criticism of *Ben Hur* lies in an arraignment of its so-called "faulty syntax." Those who make this criticism in every case fail to give any quotation in illustration of their view, or to be specific in any other way. If one were to go through *Ben Hur* hunting for irregularities of syntax, doubtless he could find them just as easily as they may be found in the work of almost any other great novelist,—and perhaps no more easily. It is doubtful if the great majority of reviewers who have criticised the syntax of *Ben Hur* have had any thorough appreciation of what syntax is. Moreover, to quote a recent work on style, by a classical scholar, who is speaking of the style of Sophocles, it seems "that liberties of this kind are not confined to any particular stage of literary history, but are mainly due to the individual bent of the writer's genius. No ancient author, however, has carried them to a greater length than Sophocles, ... he rejoices in those confusions of *syntax* ... by which one construction is suddenly merged in another."[30] Sophocles has not perished on account of irregularities of style or syntax, nor will Lew Wallace, for any such reason. The free style of *Ben Hur* is well suited to describe its ever-changing scenes. Nor is the novel to be criticised for looseness of construction. Its combination of unity and variety make *Ben Hur* in every sense a great novel suited to a portrayal of life in the Roman Empire in the time of Christ. The chariot race, the sea fight, and the disentombing of Ben Hur's mother and sister, are thrilling episodes in the world's literature; and considered as a whole, *Ben Hur* is one of the great novels of all time.

After the appearance of *Ben Hur* many "popular" novels of Roman life tend toward a greater or less imitation of Lew Wallace's great novel. There is, however, little such imitation in John W. Graham's *Neaera* (1886), a novel the author of which displays genuine scholarship. In its description of the splendor and crime of the court of Tiberius, *Neaera* depends much on the *Annals* of Tacitus, which furnishes the best source for such a description of the Rome of Tiberius. The character of the gloomy Emperor is well drawn, as are also those of Sejanus, his mistress Livia, and Lygdus, the eunuch. Domitius Afer is made prominent, and through him we learn of the methods of the Emperor and others who make use of the ruffians of the Subura to attain their ends. The banquet of Apicius, and his suicide furnish the material for a realistic description of manners.

An example of a very poor kind of "popular" historical novel is found in *The Son of a Star* (1888), by B. W. Richardson. This is a wildly fantastic romance which bears on the title page a quotation from Horace, "Ficta voluptatis causa sit proxima veris," but is certainly very far from the truth in most respects. While *The Son of a Star* makes occasional brief displays of accurate scholarship, chiefly borrowed from other novelists, its loose construction and false atmosphere make it a good example of the novel of Roman life "gone to seed." The bright, though false, coloring of this romance suggests the work of Sir Rider Haggard, which has already been excluded from consideration in this study. His *Cleopatra* appeared in the following year (1889). This date, in fact, may be said to mark the point at which the pretended novel of Roman life, with its artificial coloring, becomes separated from the true novel of Roman life.

The idea of presenting the life of Rome as a gorgeous and at times bloody spectacle, with a frequent use of the sensational, reached its greatest height in *Quo Vadis* (1895), by the Polish author, H. Sienkiewicz. This idea had appeared in the English novel of Roman life, *e. g.*, in *Salathiel* (1827), *The Gladiators* (1863), and *Ben Hur* (1880). There is no need to review *Quo Vadis* in detail here, since it is so well known; but let us establish its relation to the English novel of Roman life. It appeared after Eckstein's *Nero* (1889), and a number of English novels of Roman life of the time of Nero, and may owe some of its inspiration to these, especially to *Darkness and Dawn* (1892). But after *Quo Vadis* was translated into English (1896), its influence upon later English novels of Roman life overshadowed even that of Canon Farrar's great and more serious work. *Quo Vadis* has been translated and read in civilized lands even more widely than *Ben Hur*. These are the two novels of Roman life which have had the most widespread influence upon all subsequent novels of Roman life the world over. *Quo Vadis* adds practically no new element to the novel of Roman life, but puts certain elements which already existed into a more intensely vivid, and even lurid form,—in short, emphasizes the sensational. In its larger outlines *Quo Vadis* is reminiscent not only of *Darkness and Dawn* but of *Hypatia*. It represents the same struggle between the Christian Church and the Roman pagan world, the same triumph of Christianity. The contrast lies between the proud, voluptuous, and cruel spirit of pagan Rome and the spirit of humility and hope of the dwellers in the catacombs. A personal contrast is seen between Nero, the royal performer in the circus, and St. Peter, the fisherman who was to rule the world by his example. Other characters are those familiar to the novel of Roman life, Petronius the connoisseur in luxury, Vinicius the active young Roman noble, Lygia the beautiful Christian maiden condemned to the arena, Ursus the powerful slave, the dissolute Poppæa and members of Nero's court, Croton the athlete, Glaucus the forgiving Christian, and others too numerous to mention. The scenes of *Quo Vadis* are also familiar, much the same as those of *Darkness and Dawn*, the picture of the fire at Rome being especially fine. While the moral lesson exists in *Quo Vadis*, what Sienkiewicz did for the novel of Roman life was to portray the life of the city of Rome itself in a form absolutely irresistible to the so-called "average" reader. Realistic effect was the most important thing to the writer of *Quo Vadis*; and in preparation for the writing of a novel which should portray the life of Rome with realistic effect he traveled widely and made a thorough study of numerous Latin authors, especially those who describe the life of Rome of the first few centuries A. D. The result is that Sienkiewicz was a profound scholar; and his scholarship appears in *Quo Vadis*,—though the novel shows some instances of error, chiefly topographical error, especially in the description of the great fire. None the less *Quo Vadis* is now the novel of Roman life which shows to the greatest extent a combination of careful scholarship and popularity of appeal. By 1900, nearly 2,000,000 copies of the English translation (1896), by Jeremiah Curtin, had been sold; and the influence of the novel upon popular taste is still important, since it creates beyond a doubt in every reader's mind a desire to read further in Roman historical fiction.

The Sign of the Cross, by Wilson Barrett, appeared immediately after *Quo Vadis*, and, though very popular, is nothing but a weak and slavish imitation of Sienkiewicz's great novel. This is all that need be said of *The Sign of the Cross* as a novel, since there is nothing original about it, and its brief popularity was due entirely to the reflected splendor of *Quo Vadis*. The fact that this novel was turned into a play with some success, following the example set by the dramatization of *Ben Hur*, shows that theatrical managers realized the possibilities offered by a novel of Roman life. Unfortunately the drama of Roman life presented either on the stage or the screen, has in nearly every instance, become more a gorgeous spectacle or a sensational melodrama, than a serious drama. But the drama of Roman life is mentioned here, since it has induced many who have seen such a play to read the novel on which it was based. This was the case with *Ben Hur*, which in the form of a novel offers, I believe, a higher and stronger appeal than any dramatic production based upon it.

Another novel which definitely goes back to *Quo Vadis* for its best scenes, but is possessed of some individual merit, is *Amor Victor*, the third edition of which appeared in 1902. This novel, by Orr Kenyon, is also marked by the seriousness of purpose which underlies the sensationalism of *Quo Vadis*. It particularly resembles *Quo Vadis* in its scenes in the arena, and in showing the tremendous difference between the appalling difficulties presented to the Christian at the time of the Empire, and those which he now meets. But *Amor Victor* also shows the similarity of atrocities committed by pagans then and now. This novel seems to be the first to draw parallels between events in the past and definite, specific occurrences of the present, taken sometimes even from personal experiences. For example, the author, in describing certain almost unthinkable atrocities which occurred in the Roman arena, shows how exactly the same outrages were committed upon the Christians by the Turks shortly before he wrote. Even since *Amor Victor* was written, these scenes have been repeated in Turkey. Moreover, Kenyon, in describing the scene in which Arsaces, the giant Parthian, kills a lion in the arena, is recalling the time when he himself had seen Sandow, the famous strong man, throw a lion in a public exhibition. This definite use of an incident, which the author has seen with his own eyes, aids him in achieving realistic effect. A similar use of an incident which actually occurred, is made by Mr. E. L. White in *Andivius Hedulio* (1921), in which the description of the miraculous escape of Commodus' chariot from disaster was suggested by a real accident in the streets of Baltimore. *Amor Victor* takes its story of St. John the Apostle from the patristic writings. It is accurate in its historical coloring. In speaking of his serious purpose, the author says in a note at the end of *Amor Victor*, "Newell Dwight Hillis has shown that really great works of fiction are those which illustrate some vital principle, some deep moral lesson." The novel conveys a moral lesson. Yet, while parts of it are also written in juvenile style, *Amor Victor* is not merely a story of religious instruction, but a true novel of Roman life. *The Story of Phaedrus*, by Hillis, to which Kenyon has reference in his quotation, is more a story of religious instruction written in distinctly juvenile style. Its hero does not see much of Roman life, since he spends most of his life in copying sacred writings in the depths of the catacombs.

An imitation of *Ben Hur* with some original touches is Mr. Irving Bacheller's *Vergilius; A Tale of the Coming of Christ* (1904). The author reverses the plan of Lew Wallace, by placing the birth of Christ at the end, instead of at the beginning of his story. Mr. Bacheller's attempt to use the birth of Christ as a climax, to which the rest of the story leads, is not very successful. His treatment of sacred scenes falls far below that of Lew Wallace, and the construction of his plot is poor. But he has described some scenes in Roman life with fine realistic effect, particularly those which take place in the magnificent palaces of Rome and Jerusalem. The descriptions of intrigues which take place in the court of Augustus, show the uncertainty of life at Rome at the time. The characters are few in number, Augustus and the young Jewish prince Herod Antipater being the only important historical figures. The crafty nature of Augustus is portrayed with a very keen insight into the depths of human nature, and the vindictive hatred of the Jewish prince forms a marked contrast to the noble, ingenuous nature of Vergilius, the imaginary hero of the story. Vergilius is a young patrician, and a favorite of Augustus; his character is not idealized and is quite representative of Roman times. In justice to Mr. Bacheller's work, it should be said that he has not attempted to fill as large a canvas as did Lew Wallace in *Ben Hur*; his picture of life in Roman times is more limited in its scope, and more chaste in its outlines. Scenes which make use of the sensational are not overdone. *Vergilius* is a novel of Roman life, containing many beautifully written passages, which give it a very high position among such novels.

Lux Crucis (1904) is a very readable novel by Mr. Samuel M. Gardenhire. It is called by its author *A Tale of the Great Apostle*, and is dedicated to the Rt. Rev. Ethelbert Talbot, Bishop of Central Pennsylvania. *Lux Crucis* is, more than any other novel I know of, an attempt to portray Roman life by taking as much material as possible from previous novels of Roman life. Everything is thus taken at second-hand, without recourse to original sources. This method may show wide reading, but hardly shows thorough scholarship. Scenes in the arena depend upon *Quo Vadis*; scenes which have to do with St. Paul and Christian characters suggest *Ben Hur* and *Darkness and Dawn*; while other passages, especially that representing the gladiator's school, undoubtedly go back to *The Last Days of Pompeii*. The author takes his history, chronology, and topography at second hand, and apparently he is confused in his remembrance of his own reading. The result is that *Lux Crucis* probably contains more ridiculous mistakes than any other novel of Roman life. For example, a so-called Briton is given the Anglo-Saxon name of Ethelred, though he lives in the time of Nero, before the Saxon invasion of Britain; he is made to come from Brittany, though Armorica did not receive that name until at least six hundred years later; and he speaks of crossing the channel to Angle-land, "with a smile." (The reader also smiles.) An anachronism which is related to topography occurs, when the Forum of Trajan is mentioned in this story of Nero's time, though the accession of Trajan did not take place until thirty-three years later. These typical instances of error in *Lux Crucis* are selected from a great number, some of which are almost equally bad. It is remarkable that, in spite of these inconsistencies, the novel is pleasing in its portrayal of characters, historical and non-historical, and many of its scenes are by no means devoid of realistic effect. *Lux Crucis* furnishes examples of the pitfalls awaiting an author who has attempted a piece of work requiring scholarship, but has been handicapped by his unscholarly methods.

Mr. Walter S. Cramp's popular novel, *Psyche* (1905), describes the Rome of Tiberius, and contains much sound history taken from the *Annals* of Tacitus. In this it resembles Graham's *Neaera*, which had appeared in 1886. In 1913 Mr. Cramp published another novel of Roman life, called *An Heir to Empire*, which is much like *Psyche* in its general outlines, except that the story centers in the life of Augustus' court, instead of in the life of the court of Tiberius. It makes no great misuse of history, but adds too many fanciful details to historical episodes; this in spite of the fact that the novel is formally dedicated "To the Honorable Rodolpho Lanciani, whose genius touched the dust and ruins of Ancient Rome and made them live."

F. INFLUENCE OF FRENCH NOVELS OF ROMAN LIFE

Hitherto no mention has been made of the influence of French novels of Roman life upon English novels of Roman life. And I have found that this influence of French novels is not nearly so important as might be supposed, but on the whole, is rather an indefinite thing. But before concluding our survey of the "popular novel" of Roman life and the "gorgeous romance," it is best to say a few words, (regarding the latter phrase especially), of the influence of certain French novels. In 1862 Gustave Flaubert's famous *Salammbo* appeared in the English translation. While this great work undoubtedly had a tremendous influence as a "gorgeous romance," it is difficult to trace this influence directly. *The Gladiators* (1863) appeared the following year, and exhibits a similarity of style in presenting the gorgeous pageantry of the past; but while *The Gladiators* may owe something to *Salammbo*, it seems more likely that Whyte-Melville's novel was an independent effort to please a certain element of the public taste. Later and greater novels, such as *Ben Hur* and *Quo Vadis*, may have profited by the splendid example of Flaubert, who filled a large canvas with brilliant colors, but did not sacrifice truth,—but here again the influence is indefinite. In fact, *Salammbo* appears to have stood forth with such tremendous power that it discouraged rather than encouraged imitation. No one,—so novelists have thought,—could hope to equal Flaubert's novel in splendor of style or in realistic effect. Thus *Salammbo* has remained the only great novel whose scene is ancient Carthage. Though its scene does not go to Rome, no view of Roman life would be complete without some knowledge of the most powerful enemy of the Roman Republic, whose life was so closely connected with that of Rome. *Salammbo* combines the story of a Carthaginian princess, a sister of Hannibal, with an account of the Mercenary War. The description of this war of Carthage with her own soldiers, suggests troubles Rome later had with armies composed of heterogeneous elements. *Salammbo* is equally vivid in its description of the pagan customs of Carthage, particularly of the custom of offering human sacrifices to Moloch. A few books which describe the city life of Carthage, or her wars with the Romans, no doubt owe their inspiration indirectly to *Salammbo*. G. A. Henty's excellent book for boys, *The Young Carthaginian* (1886), describes the political organization and social conditions existing in the city of Carthage, and gives a similar description of the sacrifice to Moloch, before taking Hannibal on his campaign against Rome. *The Lion's Brood* (1901) has its scene entirely in the Italian peninsula. Recently Señor Blasco Ibañez published *Sonnica* (1920), which seems to show evidence of his reading of *Salammbo*. In this novel Hannibal's siege of the semibarbaric city of Saguntum recalls Flaubert's description of the siege of Carthage by the Mercenaries. *Sonnica*, besides giving a good characterization of Hannibal, is especially noteworthy for its accurate portrayal of the stern, bare, and crude city of Rome in the early days of the republic. This portrayal contains a fine paragraph on the Roman father, and mentions several historical characters, such as the vindictive Cato and the slave Plautus. *Sonnica* does not appear as yet to have influenced novels of Roman life in English, though it may have given some suggestions to Mr. Jaquelin A. Caskie, who has written *Nabala* (1922), an attractive novelette, dealing with the Third Punic War. More likely *Nabala*, (as everything else in fiction connected with Hannibal and Carthage before her fall seems to do), goes back for its principal inspiration to *Salammbo*. Its scenes of fighting outside the city of Carthage recall similar scenes in *Salammbo*, as does its description of what goes on inside the city, the human sacrifice to Moloch furnishing the climax of the story.

A novel written in quite different style by Flaubert is *The Temptation of St. Anthony* (1874). This has for its scene the cell of an anchorite in the time of Constantine, since St. Anthony says in the novel, "The Emperor Constantine has written me three letters." In describing the visions[31] which pass through the mind of the saint, however, the author makes it seem as though the entire pageant of the past history of the Roman Empire were passing before his eyes. In his temptation the saint sees pagan gods pass before him, and he takes on the personality of famous kings, with their unlimited power to gratify their passions. In his mental wanderings, he speaks of Athanasius, the Arians, and the monks of Nitria. This last thought recalls the part which the savage monks of Nitria play in Kingsley's *Hypatia*, and the talk of other affairs of the Church also suggests *Hypatia*. Moreover, the situation of St. Anthony alone in his cell in the desert is strongly reminiscent of passages at the beginning and the end of Kingsley's novel. But St. Anthony's strongest temptation comes in the form of the vision of Thais, an irresistibly beautiful courtesan. This suggests M. Anatole France's (Jacques Anatole France Thibault) *Thais* (1889), which also makes a portrayal of the beautiful courtesan. Custom forbids English and American novelists from making such a portrayal in detail, and it is to be doubted whether they could present such a picture with the realism of French authors, whose view-point has always been radically different, as regards the degree of frankness to be allowed a novelist in portraying a man's passion for a beautiful woman. The portrayal of the beautiful courtesan in the French novel of Roman life reaches the greatest frankness in Pierre Louys' *Aphrodite*, which is, in effect, a description of the schools of prostitution in Roman Alexandria. French novels of this kind have had little effect on novels of Roman life written in English. However, there is one novel written by an American of French descent, which frankly tells the story of a beautiful courtesan, and will now be discussed.

Mr. T. Everett Harré published in Philadelphia in 1916 *Behold the Woman*. This is the story of the famous Alexandrian courtesan of transcendent beauty, who is known in the *Lives of the Saints* as St. Mary of Egypt. Mr. Harré takes the general outlines of his story from the *Lives of the Saints*, though adding much from invention. And, while *Behold the Woman* shows an individuality of style and a remarkable power of description, it appears to be a book full of echoes. There is, for example, some similarity of plot between *Behold the Woman* and the *Thais* of M. Anatole France, in that both novels portray the repentance and regeneration of the fallen woman.

M. France in *Thais* had been said to combine "a curiously subtle piety of imagination with impiety of thought." (B. W. Wells in *The Encyclopedia Americana*, 1920.) Whether this criticism is just or not, as applied to *Thais*, it must be said most emphatically that Mr. Harré's work shows absolutely no impiety of thought. In presenting the facts of life in the Roman world, in *Behold the Woman*, he is making a simple statement of the truth. Piety of imagination is indeed displayed in the story of Mary's conversion and life of penitence in the desert. But even in such a scene as that in which the supposed room of the Lord's Supper is desecrated by the orgy of the fallen monks, the author shows no impiety of thought. Nor, if one sets aside questions of religion, and rests his faith on mere morality, can the charge of immorality be brought against *Behold the Woman* with any sincerity whatever. In certain scenes of *Behold the Woman* there appears evidence of a direct borrowing from Pierre Louys' *Aphrodite*, in which there had been an elaborate description of the bath and toilet of the courtesan, with an extensive catalogue of her charms in symbolic language. In *Behold the Woman* the scenes attending the destruction of the temple of Serapic remind one of Ebers'

Serapis, which had described similar scenes. But Mr. Harré particularly excels in describing with minute touches the superstition of the Roman soldiers, who were called upon to destroy the temple and its huge idol, but feared to do so. Moreover, the brutal conduct of the military on this occasion and at the breaking up of the banquet at Mary's palace, well represents the ruthless use of Rome's mighty power. There also appear to be in *Behold the Woman* some slight suggestions taken from Kingsley's novel, *Hypatia*, the same proper names being used, but transposed; the name of Philammon, Kingsley's hero, is given to a character in *Behold the Woman*, who corresponds to one of the minor characters in *Hypatia*. Moreover, the scenes of riot in the streets of Alexandria, which appear in *Behold the Woman*, are reminiscent of similar scenes in *Hypatia*. The two books represent the savage monks in a similar way; and Mary is able to see through their sham Christianity, just as Philammon saw through the pretenses of the monks, in *Hypatia*. But as Mr. Harré says in his preface, he does not agree with Kingsley that "one who writes of such an era cannot tell how evil people were." Here he is quoting the preface of *Hypatia*, though he does not say so. In *Behold the Woman*, he does tell how evil people were; and justly remarks in its preface that the novel is one for strong men and fearless women, not for children. The description of the orgy at the banquet in Mary's palace is perhaps as realistic a portrayal of such a scene as is made in any novel of Roman life; but the frankness of this description is certainly very nearly equaled in Canon Farrar's *Darkness and Dawn*, a novel which no one would think of calling immoral in any sense of the word. The description of Mary's sordid life in the Brucheum, the slum quarter of the city, is also realistic, and portrays a side of life which has been neglected by the authors of novels of Roman life, even when they claimed to be presenting life among all classes of society.

Other scenes in *Behold the Woman* are similar to those which are already familiar in the novel of Roman life. And no matter what he is describing, the author's genius and originality have enabled him to portray scenes from life in Roman times, with a vividness and realism hardly exceeded in any novel of Roman life. The style of *Behold the Woman* is richly ornamental at times, but never too flowery for the theme which the author has in hand. *Behold the Woman* could be placed in the class of the "gorgeous romance" along with such novels as *Ben Hur* and *Quo Vadis*. But it shows, more than any other novel of Roman life in English, the influence of the French novels of which we have spoken.

G. NOVELS WRITTEN BY TEACHERS OF ROMAN HISTORY OR OF THE CLASSICS

Some of the novels which have been mentioned were written by school teachers or college professors. Charles Kingsley at the time when he wrote *Hypatia* was a school teacher very much in need of more pupils, whose fees would help him make both ends meet.[32] The Rev. A. J. Church, M. A., to whose books for boys allusion has been made, was a Professor of Latin at University College, London. But I wish to consider now those novels which have been written by teachers, who wished especially to illustrate certain periods of Roman history, or to make the life of some great Roman historical character stand out with particular vividness. The word "novels," as here used, is meant to apply in the main to books which can be read with pleasure both by boys and their elders; and it will be recalled, that in defining the novel of Roman life, books written only for boys, or written with a religious motive, were excluded. The work of the Rev. A. J. Church is therefore excluded, practically for two different reasons. But, since it often touches closely the true novel of Roman life, the titles of some of his books will be mentioned. His *Two Thousand Years Ago* (1885) has been spoken of, as following Eckstein's *Prusias* (1884), which is also on the Spartacus theme; but Church's book is entirely a book for boys. *The Count of the Saxon Shore* (1887) is a similar book on the period marking the end of Roman control in Britain. *To the Lions* (1889) makes the same use of the correspondence between Trajan and Pliny that had been made in *Valerius*; but its scene is Bithynia, and it is purely a religious story. *The Burning of Rome* (1892), as has been said, follows Eckstein's *Nero* (1889), but even this book by Church cannot be called a novel, though it is his best book. *Lords of the World* (1898) describes the fall of Carthage and Corinth. Finally, *The Crown of Pine* (1905) tells of the banishment of the Jews from Rome in the time of Claudius, of the preaching of St. Paul, and of the Isthmian games at Corinth. The style of this last book is characteristic of the Rev. Church's work; his thorough scholarship is greater than his power to interest the reader, juvenile or otherwise.

A novel (for so it fully deserves to be called), written before the Rev. Church's books, is *Helena's Household* (1858). This is by James De Mille, Professor of Belles Lettres at Dalhousie College, N. S. Though it has been catalogued as a juvenile book, it hardly deserves this description. And while it is dedicated to the Rev. John Pryor, D. D., and shows some influence of the story of religious instruction, it deserves to be classified as a novel of Roman life. *Helena's Household* has a very good historical background, and contains some very fine descriptions of life at Rome. The story of Boadicea's defeat is told by a Briton who was taken captive on that occasion. This same Briton is made to fight in the arena, in a scene which is fairly well done. This mention of a British slave, and the outline of the siege and destruction of Jerusalem at the end of the novel, suggest *The Gladiators* (1863), a novel which resembles De Mille's book in its rambling construction. Nero's atrocities are in the main passed over, though there is a fine description of the great fire at Rome, which he is said to have caused; and the buffoon Emperor is described as acting at the games in Greece. Pomponia is not made a very important character in the story, but her Christianity is made the excuse for entirely too much religious talk, for a novel of Roman life. St. Paul and St. Luke are represented as prisoners, and a fine description is given of St. Paul's heroic death, though his martyrdom is not the central theme of the story by any means. Moreover, the life of the Christians is realistically described, without the false element of terror, which is often added to such descriptions. In spite of its rambling construction, and religious discussion, *Helena's Household* is a scholarly piece of work, which both illustrates Roman history, and portrays well the life of Rome. *The Martyr of the Catacombs*, (1858), by De Mille, is more a religious story than a novel.

A fine illustration of Roman history is given in *Kallistratus; an Autobiography* (1897), a novel dealing with the campaigns of Hannibal against Rome. This is not to be considered an imitation of Flaubert's *Salammbo*, or any other novel dealing with the Carthaginians, but is an independent attempt to illustrate certain facts of Roman history. The author of *Kallistratus* was Mr. A. H. Gilkes, M. A., Master of Dulwich College, Dulwich, and the preface to the novel is written from the College. *Kallistratus* need not be considered a book for boys, and is infinitely better than most books for boys. But its hero, Kallistratus, is a typical boys' hero, who serves as Hannibal's aide and personal attendant. Besides telling the story of the Second Punic war from Hannibal's point of view, *Kallistratus* presents with a very realistic effect an account of the chicanery of an ancient oracle, which is located on the banks of the Rhone near Massilia, and is consulted by a Gallic chieftain. Hannibal's victories over the Romans are accurately described, and attributed in part to Varro, the low-born consul, as they should be. Moreover, the fact that Kallistratus' brothers and sisters are sent to Rome under the protection of the Scipios, affords the author an opportunity to describe life at Rome to some extent. While the character of the great Hannibal does not stand out with especial force in this novel, *Kallistratus* gives a truly realistic account of his campaigns from the point of view of one who was with him; and it may well have served as a model in many ways for Mr. Duffield Osborne, when he was writing *The Lion's Brood*, (1901), a novel which treats of the same period from the Roman point of view. Mr. Gilkes' other novel, *Four Sons*, (1909), seems to lapse into more juvenile style, mainly because its subject is not so inspiring. But it illustrates very faithfully the period of Roman history which was marked by the inroads of the Greeks in Southern Italy and the Samnite War. The author's interest in books for boys and the school life of boys, is shown not only by the profession he has chosen, but also in the genuine book for boys he has written, called *Boys and Masters*. But of the books he has written, *Kallistratus* especially, would be of interest to any intelligent reader, juvenile or otherwise.

A Friend of Caesar, (1900), by William Stearns Davis, a college professor, whose scholarly attainments have won for him a well-deserved reputation, is the first and, in my opinion, the only book which successfully illustrates with the most minute detail every important event or incident in a brief period of Roman history (50-47 B. C.), crowded with important events,—and at the same time presents a fictitious story of supreme interest, surpassing that of most historical novels. It is in fact, the world's best school-history book in the form of fiction. Mr. Davis was well qualified to write such a book, by his experience in writing in briefer form stories meant to aid in the study of Roman history in schools and colleges,—his parallel readings have been widely used by other teachers. *A Friend of Caesar* is a very scholarly piece of work by a very scholarly man; and it is absolutely accurate in its history, presenting everything which a school-boy may be expected to learn in his study of Roman history and life of a definite period. Yet, while it is very slightly expurgated of grosser elements, it is in no sense a book for boys alone, but a *novel* which can satisfy the taste of the most mature readers. Mr. Davis has thus succeeded in combining, in a single volume, elements which other authors have found it very difficult to combine. *A Friend of Caesar* is in fact a novel of Roman life in the best sense in which that phrase can be used. As Mr. Davis says in his preface to the novel, "If this book serves to show that classical life presented many phases akin to our own, it will not have been written in vain." This sentence shows the highest possible conception of the function of the historical novel. In portraying life at Rome at the time of the fall of the Roman Republic, Mr. Davis (in his preface) disparages his own work in comparison with that in *Quo Vadis*; he says that he is taking the pagan point of view rather than the Christian. But, judged purely from a consideration of the necessity for accurate scholarship, *A Friend of Caesar* is a far more thorough work than *Quo Vadis*; and, while containing a number of scenes of great dramatic value, it does not rely unduly on the melodramatic and the sensational. In matters requiring minute and careful scholarship, it is possible that Mr. Davis goes too far; there are times when the reader feels that it is becoming *too much* a school-book. Yet this insistence on detail, while leading to possible faults, also assures the principal virtue of *A Friend of Caesar*, its absolute reliability.

Julius Caesar himself is the most important figure in this novel. The finest and noblest points in the character of this great man, among the world's great men, are emphasized; while his defects are entirely left out of the picture. The resulting character of Caesar in the book is thus idealized to some extent, but perhaps not too much so for the purpose of a novel. Caesar appears as the hero, great statesman, and controller of the world's destinies that he was. The technical hero of the story is Quintus Livius Drusus, and he is a typical boy's hero; his history is given in a way which arouses interest and associates him closely, in the reader's mind, with Caesar. Cleopatra seems to have been an important character in the author's mind, mainly because she played an important part in history. Her personality is viewed in a somewhat more attractive light than might be expected, and as a character she blends well with the idealized character of Caesar. The weaker side of Pompeius' character is emphasized, and he is not brought into the foreground enough to be considered a really important character. The manner of his death is well portrayed in ch. XXII, "The End of the Magnus."

Perhaps the most notable scene in *A Friend of Caesar* is the historical one in the Curia. In this the destinies of the Roman Republic are shown to be in the hands of its own unscrupulous government, just as much as they are later in the hands of Caesar; this scene is truly great, and contains no apparent inconsistencies. The scene in which Agias is saved by Fabia, is modelled somewhat on a similar scene between Onesimus and a Vestal in Canon Farrar's *Darkness and Dawn*, as Mr. Davis candidly says in his preface. The scene depicting the riot in Alexandria, especially the passage which shows how little the brutal Roman soldiers care for the lives of the poorer citizens, recalls a similar scene in *Hypatia*. But *A Friend of Caesar* contains very little direct borrowing from previous novels of Roman life, and does not rely too much upon historical events as a means of obtaining realistic effect. The scene in which trusty old Mamercus guards the door of the villa, is a masterpiece in its description of hand-to-hand fighting, and excels, in its realism, the description of the actual battle between the forces of Caesar and those of Pompey. In its portrayal of character, and its presentation of realistic scenes, *A Friend of Caesar* is a novel which rests firmly upon its own merits.

George Manville Fenn was not a teacher, but his book for boys, *Marcus, the Young Centurion*, (1904), is given passing mention here, since, like Mr. Davis's novel, it deals with Julius Caesar. Fenn's book tells something of Caesar's campaigns in Gaul, but a far better book on this subject is *The Standard Bearer; a Story of Army Life in the Time of Caesar*, (1915), by Mr. Albert Carleton Whitehead. This book tells very realistically the story given in Caesar's *Commentaries*, but is rather a book for boys than a novel of Roman life.

The Unwilling Vestal, (1918), by Mr. Edward Lucas White, a teacher and thorough scholar of Baltimore, Maryland, was quite evidently written to show that life in ancient Rome was essentially "modern." While this novel mentions historical events, such as the campaigns of Marcus Aurelius, and gives a most striking portrayal of the effects of the great pestilence at Rome, it does not attempt to narrate historical details so much, as to make the life and customs of ancient Rome seem familiar and real to the modern reader. It has achieved this latter purpose by presenting Roman life chiefly as it affects a single character, Brinnaria the Vestal. It is true that the figure of Marcus Aurelius appears in the novel, and at the close of the book Commodus plays an important part; Almo, the charioteer, is a character of whom we hear much at second-hand, but we seldom make a closer acquaintance with him, and even the descriptions of his fights in the amphitheatre are lacking in realistic effect. The Vestals, with whom Brinnaria is later associated, are given natural and human qualities, but do not play any very important part. *The Unwilling Vestal* is a character-study, a study of one character. The other characters are important only as they influence the principal one. Moreover, the varied scenes of Roman life which are portrayed center about the principal character. Hence, most of them have to do with the life of a Vestal. This is shown to be far from a narrow or confining life. In addition, the author seems justified in selecting for his Vestal a person so independent, self-willed, and unusual as Brinnaria. Her parents play little part in the story, and from the very first, she shows a disposition to "go it alone." By devoting so much attention to Brinnaria, and emphasising her human qualities, whether virtues or faults, the author has succeeded in making us feel that we know Brinnaria well. It seems to be a part of the author's purpose to convince us that Brinnaria and her chum Flexinna are not essentially different from the modern American girls we see and know; and so he gives us a thorough acquaintance with Brinnaria, the girl, before introducing us to Brinnaria, the Vestal. There are no really great scenes in *The Unwilling Vestal*. In attempting to recall any such, one thinks at once of the scenes in the amphitheatre; but here, as elsewhere, we are concerned with Brinnaria, her feelings, and her interests.

While Almo, the charioteer, comes before us directly only a few times, the story, (indirectly told), of his career as charioteer, gladiator, villicus, and King of the Grove, affords opportunity to throw interesting sidelights on things that took place here and there in the world of the Roman Empire. For example, a concise and accurate account of the way in which the racing companies were managed, is given. An interesting account is given of Brinnaria's occupations inside the Temple of Vesta, and, as has already been indicated, it is shown that, besides being a Vestal, she was an important figure in the social life of Rome. The author says:

She took great delight in mixing in society merely for society's sake. Moderns are likely to imagine that the Vestals of ancient Rome were nuns, or something like nuns. They were nothing of the sort. They were maiden ladies of wealth and position, whose routine duties brought them into familiar association with all the men important in the Roman government, hierarchy, nobility, and gentry, and with their wives and daughters.

Though *The Unwilling Vestal* fails to present some of its scenes with realistic effect, because of the lack of a sufficient number of characters of different kinds, its author does portray some very interesting things in Roman life, through the medium of a single interesting character and a very real one. Mr. T. Everett Harré had given a vivid picture of life in Roman Alexandria, while presenting only one important character, in *Behold the Woman*, (1916), two years before; but the character of Mary, while intensely human, is not intended to show especially "modern" traits of character. Brinnaria in *The Unwilling Vestal*, is made to seem in some ways more familiar to the modern reader, and more like his modern acquaintances, than any other single character in any novel of Roman life, written before Mr. White's book. Besides being an interesting novel, *The Unwilling Vestal* is so accurate in its description of Roman life and custom that it could be used as a schoolbook of great value. Finally, the so-called "modern scientific touch" is given in the crucial scene of the story, in which Brinnaria exonerates herself by carrying water in a sieve,—something which the author had seen done in a series of accurate experiments. *The Unwilling Vestal* is original in style, and does not seem to depend on previous novels of Roman life in any way. Its omission of any mention of the Christians, makes it easier for the author to portray truthfully the life of Pagan Rome.

In *The Unwilling Vestal*, (1918), Mr. White had told many interesting things about Roman life, but in limiting himself to a single important character, whose experiences are narrated in the third person, he sometimes had failed to make the reader feel a share in the life of Rome, as an eye-witness of the scene, or even a participant in it. Such a realistic effect he actually attained in *Andivius Hedulio, Adventures of a Roman Nobleman in the Days of the Empire*, (1921). This improvement he brought about in part by introducing a large number of characters from all ranks and conditions of Roman society, thus "presenting, in a narrative fiction, a complete and faithful depiction of all the phases, high and low, of that life which made up the grandeur which was Rome."[33] And most of the numerous characters are made just as familiar to the reader as Brinnaria had been made in *The Unwilling Vestal*. But this is not the only means taken by the author to make his novel realistic; and the realistic effect is made complete by the fact that the adventures of Hedulio are narrated in the first person by a character who has the entire sympathy of the reader. While not a great believer in newspaper reviews, I am willing to admit there is some justice in the high praise made by "G. W. D." in *The Evening Public Ledger*, Philadelphia. After comparing *Andivius Hedulio* to *Salammbo*, he says of Mr. White's novel, "The history is so subtly interwoven with the narrative, that it becomes an integral part of it. The attention of the reader is concentrated on the human relations and the characters are men and women kin with the men and women of the present century. Mr. White has made the past live as if it were the present. Or to put it another way, he has abolished time, and has exhibited to us the unchanging human emotions playing upon one another in Rome of the second century, just as they play upon one another in America of the twentieth century. He has not once yielded to the temptation to display his eruditions at the expense of the story, a temptation to which so many learned men succumb when they try to write historical fiction. They succumb because they lack the instinct of the story teller, and do not realize that a novel must be a human drama first, whatever else it may be, whether a study of manners or of morals or a picture of the world in a historical epoch.... There is nothing that people are more interested in than in other people."

Any adverse criticism of *Andivius Hedulio* would most naturally be directed against the somewhat loose construction of its plot. The plot of the novel imagines the young Roman nobleman wrongly suspected of conspiring against the life of the Emperor Commodus. Fleeing for his life, he passes eleven years in various disguises, never getting very far from Italy and returning again and again to Rome, through one chance or another. As the author says in his *Note to the Reader*, "The plot ... has a general resemblance to the ancient *Milesian* tales; as, for instance, that on a version of which Shakespeare based his *Comedy of Errors*. More definitely it is affiliated with the plot of the *Metamorphoses* of Apuleius... Much of the plot shows derivation from romances of the *Picaresco* type, or approaching that type... The atmosphere of the adventures collectively is indubitably that of the *Satiricon* of Petronius, along with much from the *Metamorphoses* of Apuleius." Much of the plot, says Mr. White, came from his assuming that there was a fashionable litter-craze at Rome, "a fad of wealthy fops for journeying by litter instead of by travelling coach... Much of the minor incident and local color derives from my saturating myself with what survives to us of Roman roadbooks." In a sense *Andivius Hedulio is* a romance of the road. In reading the novel, I was much impressed by the author's genuine delight in strange, unexpected, but *not improbable* adventures, and was reminded much of certain aspects of the romances of Robert Louis Stevenson; it was no surprise to discover later that I had overlooked its dedication "To Robert Louis Stevenson, who in reading fiction loved 'The open road and the bright eyes of danger.'" Moreover Mr. White, like Stevenson, realized that the best way to tell a story, especially a story of adventure, is to tell "one thing after another." This is the way it was done by the authors of the *Milesians*, of the *Metamorphoses*, and of the "picaresque" romances. Such works have their place in the line of ancestry of the modern novel, and the author is entirely justified in using them,— somewhat expurgated,—since often they portray life in a very realistic way. It cannot be said that *Andivius Hedulio* excels such great novels as *Ben Hur* and *Darkness and Dawn*, in portraying the life of the Roman world with realistic effect. But the author's genius, in making the experiences of characters of the Roman world seem essentially like our own experiences, and those of our friends, makes this novel excel most other novels of Roman life in this respect.

Andivius Hedulio is the work of a scholarly teacher of Latin, who wished to throw a strong light on the life of the historical period of Commodus' reign; and especially to present Commodus in the character of "the most perfect athlete the world ever produced, misplaced on earth's greatest throne." Mr. White's novel is in no sense a school-history book, such as Mr. Davis's *A Friend of Caesar*; but any school-boy could read it with pleasure, and learn from its sound scholarship, much, that would aid him in his classical studies. Commodus is the most important historical figure, and, as the author says, the part he plays in the novel is due in part to what is said of him in the work of Gibbon, Dio Cassius, and Herodian. While other sources mentioned by Mr. White in his *Note to the Reader*, show a wide reading and a thoroughness of scholarship, the novel itself is sufficient evidence of this, and is entirely free from slavish copying. He frankly admits that the culminating incident in the chariot races originated partly from certain details in the chariot race in *Ben Hur*, (1880). But this incident is given a peculiar originality, by the addition of details taken from the account given to Mr. White of a "run away" accident, which actually occurred in Baltimore. This illumination of the past, by placing in a story of the past an incident which has recently occurred, often aids a novelist in attaining realistic effect, and illustrates one of the ways Mr. White has taken to make the past seem real to present-day readers. The labyrinth motive appears in *Andivius Hedulio*, when the hero and his faithful servant make their escape from a secret stair, and through a long, dark and filthy drain. This incident was suggested by the escape of Jean Valjean in Victor Hugo's *Les Miserables*, and Baring-Gould may have taken a similar incident in *Perpetua* from the same source.

Commodus' joy in driving his horses to victory in the chariot races and in displaying his skill in the amphitheatre, is well portrayed by the author, but perhaps the greatest stroke in the portrayal of Commodus, is made, not when he is governing horses, or overcoming single opponents, animal or human, in the arena, but when he is controlling the minds and passions of the army of mutineers. While Commodus is not the technical hero of the story, he is the real hero of the novel, and in a fine character-study he is represented as the man who really controlled the Roman world, whether addressing soldiers and courtiers, or impressing the populace by his skill in the arena. But besides presenting life at the court of Commodus and in the higher social circles at Rome, with which the Emperor was definitely connected, the novel takes one through the streets of Rome and into different quarters of the city, in such a way as to illustrate the life of all classes of Roman society; and presents with fairness most of the various types of human character, which were to be found in the city of Rome itself and in various parts of the Empire. Since the Christians were comparatively few in number, even as late as the time of Commodus, (and the life of Rome was still essentially pagan), the author wisely refrains from any attempt to give them a place in his story. He says of

Andivius Hedulio, "Especially I judged it free from vital anachronisms. I know of no fiction dealing with Rome or Greece which does not project-back later ideas of duty, right and wrong, morality and such like ethical concepts, into periods far anteceding those in which these conceptions developed. The Greeks and Romans had very definite notions as to personal morals, decency, duty, and the like, but many of the ideas most prevalent among us originated since Roman times and were then non-existent and inconceivable." It would be beside the mark to cry "paganism," against Mr. White's *Andivius Hedulio*, since paganism is exactly what he wished to portray. In some respects this novel excels any other previously discussed, in its portrayal not only of the outward life, but of the *social* and *ethical* atmosphere of pagan Rome. And its teacher-author has been eminently successful in showing, to school-boy and mature reader alike, "all the phases, high and low, of that life which made up the grandeur which was Rome."

H. NOVELS WRITTEN BY AUTHORS WHO HAVE PORTRAYED ROMAN LIFE FROM AN ESTHETIC VIEWPOINT

Walter Pater's *Marius the Epicurean* appeared in 1885. While Pater was a tutor at Oxford, *Marius the Epicurean* is so far removed from being a school-book, that it was impossible to consider it in the class of novels written by teachers to illustrate Roman life or a certain period of Roman history in a pedagogical way. In fact Pater's work is so different from most novels of Roman life, and has a literary value so much higher than most novels of any kind, that it is best considered in a class by itself. Nothing has ever been written exactly like *Marius the Epicurean*, which ranks above Pater's other literary productions, fine as they are, and furnishes his principal contribution to posterity. It was indeed written for posterity, and not intended to be read as an interesting novel and then forgotten. Marius the Epicurean is the finest piece of pure literature that will be considered in this study. Moreover it cannot escape consideration as a novel of Roman life. Its full title is *Marius the Epicurean, His Sensations and Ideas*. Its hero is a Roman boy, who advances in years, until he arrives at mature manhood, and whose death is recorded at the end of the story. "It would probably have been called a novel had its chief claim and merit not been independent of fiction."[34] In following the development of Marius, Pater is showing what might have happened to a young man in the Rome of Marcus Aurelius, if he were possessed of a particularly fine esthetic sense, and devoted his life to an esthetic ideal. There is sufficient binding material in the form of narrative to make *Marius the Epicurean* rather a novel than a series of essays, though it contains fine studies of the physical and spiritual life of Rome. Such novels of Roman life as George Gissing's *Veranilda*, (1904), and Mr. Eden Phillpotts' *Pan and the Twins*, (1922), have derived much inspiration from both the substance and quality of Pater's work. Such a thorough classical scholar and ardent lover of the classics as Lionel Johnson could say of its exactness, in *Post Liminium*: "Readers, accustomed by long experience to use *Marius* for a text-book,—exact, precise, rigorous, well warranted and attested,—of the Antonine age, do not need to be told that Mr. Pater never writes without his facts and evidences."[35]

Pater's aim in *Marius the Epicurean* had something in common with the aim of some of the best novels of Roman life, that have been considered, however unique his method may have been. He purposes to show a young man in an age similar to our own, and one who exhibited "a sort of religious phase possible for the modern mind." Marius is like Pater in his serious and refined nature, and his esthetic delight in religious ceremonial, but represents better Pater's ideal. Though he is taught to believe in the outworn system of paganism, he takes delight only in the most beautiful elements in pagan religious ceremonials. In his quest of the fine and the beautiful in religious emotion, he is led to higher and higher forms of philosophy, each step in his development being minutely described by Pater, not with the accompaniment of abstract philosophizing, but with the desire to portray in simple terms the beauty of esthetic experience. At each step toward a higher intellectual existence Marius approaches the ideal of a Christian life; his soul is said to be "naturally Christian," and he admires elements of beauty in the thought and life of a Christian comrade. Finally by a mere accident, he dies a Christian. *Marius the Epicurean* simply portrays the life of Rome, as it appeared to a young Roman who lived only to seek the highest good in esthetic experience. It clearly shows that life governed by an esthetic ideal, could and did exist in the days of Marcus Aurelius, just as it can and does exist today.

In *Marius the Epicurean*, Pater, as the author, shows himself to be more a true Hellenist than any writer appears to be in any novel of Roman life written before Pater's work,—though his truly Greek appreciation of the beautiful is in no way inconsistent with Christianity. But the book portrays not merely the beauty of Greek philosophy. Viewed as a portrayal of life, *Marius the Epicurean* may be fairly said to portray essentially the entire course of the religious life of Rome,—starting with the primitive and patriarchal "religion of Numa," and passing through later forms, (whether wholly Roman or including foreign elements); and further on through the abstractions of Greek philosophy, to the highest form of Christianity. The social and moral phenomena to be seen at Rome in the times of Marcus Aurelius, are shown, and the part which great schools of Greek philosophy played in the life of Rome, is made to appear important.

While no great character portrayals are attempted in *Marius the Epicurean*, Marius is made to meet with such great characters as the Emperor Marcus Aurelius, Apuleius, and Lucian. Marcus Aurelius is portrayed in a very modern light as a public lecturer, through whose example Marius determines to become a student of rhetoric at Rome; yet to Marius he seemed to be, (as he actually was), the greatest thinker and the greatest man of his time. In his representation of the character of Faustina, who is seen surrounded by her children, including the supposedly illegitimate Commodus, Pater may owe something to Swinburne's poem, *Faustine*. Roman customs are well represented, when we see people performing sacrifices or going to the theatre to celebrate a holiday; and the life of Rome is made to seem real by minute descriptive touches, such as those which describe the evidences of the ravages of the great pestilence. Roman shops, inns, temples, and other buildings appear crowded with people, and a multitude of human types are shown, as soldiers, courtesans, beggars and little children. Some description is also made of a Roman marriage ceremony; and the mythological burlesques and gladiatorial contests of the amphitheatre are described as affecting different individuals in different ways. In the death of Verus appears something of the spirit which made the Romans turn such a matter into a public event; the great Galen, making his way through the throng to the side of the sufferer, is a figure which is familiar elsewhere in the novel of Roman life.

But the most characteristic scenes taken from the outward life of the Romans' are the banquet and the Triumph of Marcus Aurelius. Pater adds to the reality of these Roman scenes by portraying not only the characteristics of men, but also those of children, and even animals. Thus in the triumphal procession go "the ibex, the wild-cat, and the reindeer stalking and trumpeting grandly." Though scenes of the martyrdom of the Christians only appear as told at second-hand, a characteristic Roman brutality is shown by the guards in charge of Christian prisoners. Thus the material life of Rome, as well as its religious life, is portrayed in *Marius the Epicurean*. What Pater did for the novel of Roman life was to show the possibility of portraying not merely the material existence of the Romans, but the whole life of Rome considered from a religious and esthetic standpoint. *Marius the Epicurean* has been said to stand without fiction; but the highest hope of any fiction might well be to rise to the level of Pater's work. It took five or six years to write, and shows Pater's thorough scholarship, and his appreciation of the beautiful in Latin and Greek literature. Mr. Edward Hutton sums up its excellence when he says that, "In *Marius the Epicurean*, Pater gave us a book profound and simple, bounded by the great refusals of an artist, perfect in prose, stooping to nothing, having the dignity of a great poem, and the thoughtfulness that is characteristic of the writers of the Augustan age."

George Gissing in *Veranilda*, (1904), seems to be the first author of a novel of Roman life to derive much inspiration from Pater's *Marius the Epicurean*, (1885). Gissing resembles Pater in his exact scholarship, his love of Greek things, and his estheticism. *Veranilda* was to have in it the love of the classics, but is unfinished. Yet it is evident that only a few chapters at the end are missing, and what we have of *Veranilda* is finished with Gissing's finest and most delicate touches. The late Mr. Frederic Harrison says of Gissing in the preface to *Veranilda*, that in this novel, "his poetical gift for local color, his subtle insight into spiritual mysticism and, above all, his really fine scholarship and classical learning had ample field." Mr. Harrison considers *Veranilda* "far the most important book which George Gissing ever produced," and most readers of Gissing will concur in this opinion. Though the subject-matter of *Veranilda* is somewhat different from that of *Marius the Epicurean*, there is much similarity between the two books in the way subjects are presented, and at times Gissing's purity of style approaches that of Pater. In many respects *Veranilda* is the greatest novel of its kind. Not only does it show thoroughness and accuracy in scholarship, but it has very genuine characterization and atmosphere. The spirit of *Veranilda* is the spirit of the time it describes,—the spirit of disillusion, unrest, and uncertainty amid scenes of strife, sorrow, and decay. Yet there are gleams of hope to be found in Gissing's great novel, which portrays life in and near Rome in the "Era of Justinian." While the outward, physical life of fallen Rome is portrayed accurately, as it would appear to the eye, the special excellence of *Veranilda* lies in its exact reproduction of the spirit of the time with which it deals. In this respect it probably excels any other historical novel in English,—bar none,—and deserves a high position as pure literature. Moreover in his portrayal of life in the past, Gissing has not failed to establish its connection with life of the present; realistic effect is never lacking in *Veranilda*. Yet even when portraying life in the most general terms, Gissing continually shows the same selection and preference for the esthetic, the same search for the beautiful, which marks the work of Walter Pater in *Marius the Epicurean*.

The plan of *Veranilda* is more complete than that of most historical novels; it deals chiefly with real historical characters and actual historical events, yet there is not too much formal history in the novel. It was carefully written after a most thorough study of the best modern writers, (especially Gibbon), who deal with the age of Justinian and Belisarius, and of the remains of the literature of the time. The scene is Rome and Central and Southern Italy, and local color is obtained not at second-hand, but from the author's direct observation of the places he describes, and a careful review of extant documents concerning them. Gissing had spent some time travelling in Italy and *Veranilda* may be considered his most original novel. In selecting the scene and the time of *Veranilda*, Gissing evidently intended to write a novel which should convey a sense of Rome's former greatness. The center and source of power of the Roman Empire had shifted to Constantinople, though even here the power of Rome was none too strong. Felix Dahn's two novels, *A Struggle for Rome*, (1876), and *The Scarlet Banner*, (1894), deal with the same period with which *Veranilda* deals; *The Scarlet Banner* being concerned with the overthrow of the Vandal king, Gelimer, by Belisarius. *A Struggle for Rome*, is like *Veranilda* in its subject matter, since it is concerned with the struggle between the Ostrogoths and Belisarius, and mentions some of the same characters that appear in *Veranilda*. The characterization of Totila, the Gothic king, especially suggests *Veranilda*. But while *A Struggle for Rome* is Dahn's greatest novel, it does not appear that Gissing was so much indebted to it in *Veranilda*, as to original historical sources. The period with which *Veranilda* deals comes somewhat after the true end of Pagan Rome, and no novel will be discussed which deals with a later period.

Gissing preserves a fine unity of effect in making the events of his story center about Rome, and not about Constantinople. "The Eternal City" lies there as of old, and its inhabitants cannot shake off the feeling that it still is "eternal." The wise Justinian is to them a foreign tyrant, under whose governor they are harshly oppressed. The great commander Belisarius, though he has temporarily defeated the Goths, has now left Italy, and is no longer thought of as deliverer of Rome; the fame of Totila is spreading. Throughout this book, with its descriptions of ruined towns, ruined families, and the ruins of the City of Rome itself, one feels the former greatness of Rome. Everywhere is decay, everywhere is to be seen a dying out of the best elements of Roman civilization. Many of the scenes which form the setting for the principal action in the story, are typical of this lingering death of the great city. While everywhere the old Rome is dying out, is there springing up anything new to take its place? Even though the novel is incomplete, one can see that the author means to show conclusively that the Goths will furnish new life, and new strength, to Rome and to civilization.

In *Hypatia*, Kingsley had portrayed "the dying world" of Rome, especially in the chapter headed by that phrase. In *Marius the Epicurean*, Pater had pointed out the coming downfall of Rome in several different ways. He had said, for example, that the Germanic tribes, whom Marcus Aurelius defeated, were merely the advance guard of a vast body of wandering tribes destined to overrun the Roman world. Marcus Aurelius in his triumph over the Germans, appeared to Marius, "chiefly as one who had made the great mistake," as a man who had failed. "The most Christian" Stoic Emperor, in pursuing his thoroughly Roman policy of enforcing worship of the gods with an iron hand at Rome, and ruthlessly subjugating peoples on the frontiers of the Empire, had failed to save Rome from becoming more and more a nation of "coarse, vulgar people," an Empire that failed. In *Veranilda* we see the impressive remains of that great failure. Its psychology, like that of most of

Gissing's work, is the psychology of failure. As the decayed condition of his old home appears to be symbolic of failure to Marius, near the end of *Marius the Epicurean*, so all through *Veranilda* the decay of material things seems to symbolize the downfall and death of "Eternal Rome." Yet the gleams of hope, which appear through the gloom, are symbolic of a new life. While no such large contrast is made in *Veranilda*, as is made in *Hypatia*, the hope of Christianity in a failing world is made very real.

Aside from the scene depicting the murder at the villa, there are few sensational scenes in *Veranilda*. Moreover, in most of the scenes of importance, it is noticeable that only a limited number of people appear. The greater part of the novel is pitched in a minor key. There are countless incidents of importance, whisperings, doubts, uncertainties; trivial words often have a hidden meaning, trifling actions assume great importance. The remains of Rome's grandeur are suggested in the character of Flavius Anicius Maximus, a worthy descendant of an ancient and noble family; and his sister Petronilla serves to keep before our minds something of the uncompromising pride of any descendant of an old Roman family. A similar pride appears in the characters of the Deacon Leander and Vigilius. But more fitting messengers of God are the holy Abbott Benedict and his monks. The scenes about the monastery are drawn with a masterful touch; one feels the genuine influence for good, which the holy Abbott has over Basil, and the real help which he gives to Basil, in the difficulty with which Basil is confronted. St. Benedict appears as a man who leads a genuinely spiritual life, with insight enough to solve all of Basil's difficulties.

Veranilda herself is a truly radiant figure, and it is in justice that the novel is named for her. She does not often appear upon the scene, it is true, but the sincerity of her character and her overwhelming loveliness are drawn with convincing strokes. Her innocence at all times, especially when in Marcian's power, and her faith in those into whose care she is entrusted, are points of strength in her character, not of weakness; and she proves herself truly great in her forgiveness of Basil. In his delineation of character especially, Gissing has at times equalled the exquisite touches of Pater. How little is told of St. Benedict or of Veranilda, yet how definitely their characters are impressed upon the reader! Veranilda is beyond question, the character who best represents beauty of body and soul, in the novel of Roman life, and, I believe, surpasses Pater's Marius in representing a "soul naturally Christian." In any case, one feels that in *Veranilda*, as in *Marius the Epicurean*, there always exists the esthetic conception of an inseparable connection between physical and spiritual beauty. Gissing followed Pater in showing that the life of Rome could be portrayed as being far from entirely physical and material; and he showed more definitely than Pater, that Roman life could be presented in the form of a novel, with realistic effect, yet with the exercise of a discriminating selection of the finer elements of subject matter, and in a style delicately fitted to portray these finer elements.

A review of esthetic elements to be found in the novel of Roman life would not be complete without some consideration of two recent novels by Mr. Eden Phillpotts, *Evander*, (1919), and *Pan and the Twins*, (1922). Mr. Phillpotts has shown his appreciation for classic art in *The Joy of Youth*, while another of his novels, *The River*, shows his love for the beautiful in nature. Mr. George Moore says, "Morality is but a dream, but beauty is real;" his novel, *The Brook Kerith*, is not considered here as a novel of Roman life, but in it the author often harks back to the beautiful pagan world. There is something of this in the two novels of Roman life written by Mr. Phillpotts. As has been said, George Ebers had written, *A Question; The Idyl of a Picture by His Friend Alma Tadema*, (1881), which presents the beauties of pastoral life in semi-mythological classic times in pre-historic Sicily, and suggests *Evander* in subject matter. In *Marius the Epicurean*, Pater had said, "Farm life in Italy, including the culture of the olive and the vine, has a grace of its own, and might well contribute to the production of an ideal dignity of character, like that of nature itself in this gifted region. Vulgarity seemed impossible." The ideal beauty of a simple, outdoor life, centering in the farmer's hut, appears in *Evander*, a novel which portrays life in prehistoric Italy and abounds in beautiful pastoral description. In its portrayal of life, *Evander* shows somewhat the same discriminating selection of esthetic elements to be seen in *Marius the Epicurean*. and *Veranilda*; but unlike the work of Pater or Gissing, *Evander* has a rich and picturesque humor. Here, in Mr. Phillpotts' novel, is optimism in contrast to the detachment of Pater, and Gissing's somewhat continuous pessimism. Mr. Phillpott's light, humorous, cheerful style in *Evander*, makes the novel rank far below *Marius the Epicurean* and *Veranilda* as a work of art, and is a concession to popular taste; yet it has a virtue of its own. Many readers, who would find *Marius the Epicurean* too serious, could read *Evander* with pleasure and profit.

Evander portrays life in Italy when marriage was just coming into fashion; it is really a satire of the "triangle" of the ordinary man, the genius, and the woman who does not know her own mind. But it truthfully represents the beginnings of things most characteristically Roman; especially the Roman ideals of the home, the community, and finally law, ideals which sprang from the simple, austere, agricultural life of the prehistoric Romans. The author is right in representing as real to these primitive Romans, "nymphs, goat-foot fauns and other immortal creatures of lake and mountain, vale and forest, who spied upon humanity with wonder when the world was young." Among other gods, Pan, under the Latin name of Faunus, appears to a mortal woman, in *Evander*, as he had done in Mr. James Stephens' novel, *The Crock of Gold*; and the humorous, delicately satiric style of *Evander* at times suggests

Mr. Stephen's work. In portraying life "when the world was young," the author of *Evander* seems to ask, "Why should it grow old?" And in portraying ancient pagan life as a satire on modern life, he does not fail to show that the ideals and aspirations of man have changed but little.

Pan and the Twins, (1922), as its title suggests, makes a similar use of the god Pan, and is a novel written in a style similar to that of *Evander*. It differs from Mr. Phillpotts' other novel of Roman life in including historical material. Not very much history is brought into *Pan and the Twins*, but when historical events are mentioned, they are made vividly significant, and are rightly interpreted. The scene is laid chiefly on a country estate near Rome, and in the time of Valentinian, though other Roman Emperors are mentioned. Even more than *Evander*, *Pan and the Twins* suggests Mr. James Stephens' *The Crock of Gold*, but is a better constructed novel and a finer piece of art. The satire of *Pan and the Twins* is delicate but very pointed at times, as when Theodosius convinces the Christian bishop that it is not his duty to the State to have Arcadius burned alive. Its humor is equally delicate, but no one could fail to laugh at the spectacle of one of the Emperor's favorite bears, which escapes from its cage at the amphitheatre and becomes very much worried that "malefactors" are no longer provided as its daily food.[36]

While its philosophy is at times "sugar-coated," *Pan and the Twins* offers a very strong plea for sanity in religion and life, and suggests that they are one and the same thing. Moreover, in its portrayal of life, it distinctly seeks for elements of beauty. With a few delicate touches, the author presents in his heroine a figure of ideal physical and spiritual beauty, not unlike Gissing's Veranilda in conception. In portraying Roman life, coarser elements are kept in the background. One is made to feel the existence of the horrors of the amphitheatre, the inconsistencies of the Church, and much of the varied life of Rome. Roman customs, as, for example, the marriage ceremony, are correctly described. But in the foreground of the picture appear always scenes amid the sunlight and pure air of the Roman country landscape. *Pan and the Twins* is not a great novel, but one that contains much beautiful writing. The scenes which it portrays are selected chiefly for their esthetic appeal, but are real, none the less; not inconsistent with life, past or present. It is not necessarily either "pagan" or Christian; but seems to undertake to show that beauty cannot be defined entirely in terms of morality, Christianity, or paganism. *Pan and the Twins* ranks far below such a consummate piece of art as *Marius the Epicurean*, but successfully presents the esthetic, in terms more readily appreciated by the popular taste.

IV
IN CONCLUSION

In thus reviewing the principal lines of development which the novel of Roman life has followed to the present day, it has been found that, in some cases, these lines lead away ultimately from the true type of the novel which portrays the life of Rome with realistic effect. Thus the line of the novel of Roman life as written by scholarly preachers has been found to branch off, at a certain point, into the line of the story of religious instruction, a form which was excluded by definition in Section I of this study. The line of the "popular" novel of Roman life has always had a tendency to branch off, and deteriorate into cheap imitations, which attempt to use Roman life to provide artificial coloring, but do not really portray Roman life at all. The line of the novel of Roman life written to illustrate "schoolbook" history has in most cases branched off directly into the line of books for boys—Mr. Davis's and Mr. White's novels being the notable exceptions. While there has been little direct imitation of the pedantic elements in the work of German scholars, with their meticulous overemphasis upon detail; German novelists such as Eckstein have been shown to follow Scott in their methods of writing historical novels, and to suggest in turn to English novelists, the thorough way in which subjects taken from Roman life may be presented by any novelist. Few English novelists have attained notable success in portraying Roman life in terms which suggest the purity of style and beauty of thought of Pater's *Marius the Epicurean*.

The two English novels of Roman life, which have had the most profound influence upon other English novels of Roman life, are Kingsley's *Hypatia* and Wallace's *Ben Hur*; and one must look to these two especially, in any attempt to trace the lines of development which are of the most supreme importance, in the English novel of Roman life. Since the publication of these two books, *Quo Vadis* has had a very important effect upon the English novel of Roman life, but this book followed Canon Farrar's *Darkness and Dawn*, which in turn followed Eckstein's *Nero*. The importance of *Hypatia* and *Ben Hur*, in the development of the novel of Roman life, is due principally to the clear relation which they establish between the life of the Roman world and the life of today, and to their illustration of eternal truths. It must be emphasized that novels such as these give one a comprehensive idea of life throughout the Roman world; *Ben Hur* is most successful in this, but the scenes in *Hypatia*, though chiefly laid in Alexandria, are symbolic of Roman life in a larger sphere. A few novels of Roman life have attained, in some measure, the success of *Hypatia* and *Ben Hur*, by portraying life in a number of different parts of the Roman world. But most novelists have done better work by limiting the scene of their novels to the vicinity of the City of Rome itself, while not attempting work upon such large outlines as those upon which the work of Charles Kingsley and Lew Wallace is based. It has been found that novels whose scene is laid chiefly outside of and apart from any great city of the Roman world,—especially those whose scene is in one of the remote provinces of the Roman Empire,—do not really portray Roman life. This has been found to be the case with novels whose scene is Roman Britain, since they merely present very elementary illustrations of school-book history, and do not portray the life of Rome at all.

In general, the novel of Roman life has been found to be a very elastic form, and this has necessitated a certain looseness of structure in the section treating of its development, (Sec. III); but especial care has been taken not to omit significant elements in this development, and not to set up arbitrary standards of value. The principal lines of development, which the novel of Roman life has followed, and which I have endeavored to trace carefully, have not converged up to the present time; this study has therefore been devoted to an analysis of important individual elements, rather than to an attempt to construct from these elements a complete whole, based upon any abstract theory, and having a merely superficial unity. All elements of permanent value in the novel of Roman life have been given an entirely thorough consideration, the combination of a number of important elements in great novels has been pointed out; but the possibility of a further combination of these important elements into an even greater novel of Roman life than any which has yet been written, is something which the future alone can realize. While, for the sake of completeness, it has been necessary to review a number of inferior novels; these have, in most cases, been used to illustrate definite tendencies in particular lines of development of the novel of Roman life; or to mark the exact points at which such particular lines of development pass outside the limits of the field of the true novel of Roman life.

It is sincerely hoped that this study will serve as a complete and unbiased review of all the best work that has been done in the novel of Roman life. This work has been shown to be one requiring scholarship of the highest order, and offering to the reader products, whose literary merit compares favorably with that of the best work produced in other departments of the historical novel. In portraying life in the past with realistic effect, the novel of Roman life has been shown to be a direct development of the historical novel, a literary form which has in all important respects followed the example of Sir Walter Scott, and which has continued to show evidences of vigor and power to the present time. The life of ancient Rome has been shown to offer to the English historical novelist a field rich in material which illustrates the vital connection between the life of the past and the life of the present.

FOOTNOTES

[1] *Evander*: Mr. Eden Phillpotts, (1919).

[2] e. g., *A Friend of Caesar*: Mr. William Stearns Davis, (1900).

[3] *Princess Salome*: Dr. Burris Jenkins, Lippincott, Phila., (1921).

[4] *Pomponia, the Gospel in Caesar's Household*: Mrs. J. B. Peploe Webb, (1867), (Presbyterian Publication Company, o. p.).

[5] Emma Leslie in *Sowing Beside All Waters*, etc., furnishes a clear example of the most worthless kind of work to be found in the form of the story of religious instruction.

[6] Scott rarely made a great historical character *the central figure* of a novel. An exception is seen in the character of Queen Mary in *The Abbot*.

[7] *Prefatory Letter* to *Peveril of the Peak*.

[8] Scott's *Introduction* to *Ivanhoe*.

[9] Mr. Borden's list of novels of Roman life by foreign authors is:

Nero: Ernst Eckstein, (1889)

A Thorny Path: George Ebers, (1892)

Quo Vadis: H. Sienkiewicz, (1895)

The Death of the Gods: D. Merejkowski, (1901)

[10] *The Progress of Romance* (1785).

[11] *General Preface* to the *Waverly Novels*.

[12] For a more complete outline of the tendencies of the romance at this time, see *The Development of the English Novel*: Wilbur L. Cross.

[13] This motive is used in Mr. E. L. White's *Andivius Hedulio*, and in Baring-Gould's *Perpetua*; in each of these novels the hero makes his escape through the drain.

[14] Thomas Love Peacock said *The Epicurean* was "not faithful to ancient manners, and ignorant of Epicureanism."

[15] The date 1827 is given in the publisher's note to the 1901 edition, as the date when *Salathiel* was first published. This is evidently a mistake on the part of the publishers (Messrs. Funk and Wagnalls), since 1829 is given as the original date of publication by historians of the novel (*e. g.*, George

Saintsbury in *The English Novel*), and in biographical accounts of Croly (*e. g.*, *The Dictionary of National Biography*, etc.).

[16] Josephus is the direct source usually, and always the ultimate source of all novels which take the siege of Jerusalem for their theme. *cf.* Whyte-Melville's *The Gladiators*.

[17] Croly's classical scholarship is especially well displayed in his *Catiline*, which tells in the form of a verse drama the story of the famous conspiracy against the Roman republic.

[18] Since Bulwer wrote for many years under this name, before he became the Earl of Lytton, it is quite permissable to use the shorter form of his name.

[19] The scene of *Valerius*, of course, opens in Britain, but nothing of importance to the story happens there. This is doubtless a mere device to arouse the interest of English readers in the hero by hinting at the connection of "Roman" Britain with Rome.

[20] The date 1840, given in some guides to historical fiction, has been found to be incorrect.

[21] *Hypatia* was begun as a serial in Fraser's Magazine in 1851.

[22] In regard to Kingsley's choice of Hypatia for his heroine, it should be said that she typifies the last adherent of Greek philosophy, and this is the real reason she is chosen. There is, however, a marked similarity between Kingsley's heroine and Ware's Zenobia. Both were women who aspired to power, independent of the Roman government; and both conceived the idea of relying on male counselors. Hypatia, in speaking of Philammon, says: "If I could but train him into a Longinus, I could dare to play the part of a Zenobia, with him as counselor... And for my Odenatus—Orestes?" She did indeed attempt to follow this plan, even forming an alliance with Orestes, whom she detested. But even if Kingsley's heroine was in part suggested to him by Ware's Zenobia, this is not to be considered an important reason leading to the writing of *Hypatia*.

[23] For this aspect of the Oxford conspiracy, see George Borrow's *Lavengro*, (1851), and *The Romany Rye*, (1857); also W. L. Cross, *The Development of the English Novel*, p. 211, and W. L. Gates, *Essay on Newman*, in *Three Studies in Literature*, N. Y., (1899).

[24] These quotations are all from the same letter, which may be found in *Charles Kingsley; His Letters and Memories of His Life*, edited by his wife: Scribners, N. Y., 1894, abridged from the London Edition.

[25] Quoted from a notice of the English translation by M. J. Safford. The notice appeared in a contemporary number of *The Spectator*, St. Louis.

[26] From a contemporary review in *The Mail and Express*, N. Y.

[27] Among authors cited are Virgil, Pliny the Elder, Martial, Cicero, Seneca, St. Jerome, Juvenal, Tacitus, Plautus, Dion Cassius, Aulus Gellius, Aurelius Victor, Suetonius, Ovid, Ammianus Marcellinus, Tertullian, and a number of others.

[28] Wallace owes little in the chariot-race scene to Quinton's *The Money God*, though a similar scene in *The Money God* has been pointed out.

[29] Arthur Hobson Quinn, Professor of English and (former) Dean of the College, University of Pennsylvania, in *The American Novel—Past and Present; Lectures by the Faculty*, 1913-14, p. 302.

[30] J. M. Murray, *The Problem of Style*, (1922); quoted in *The Classical Weekly* February 26, 1923.

[31] *The Temptation of St. Anthony* is probably the best example of dream literature in the world, and Mr. E. L. White may have had in mind this method of transporting one's thoughts to the past, when he was collecting material for *Andivius Hedulio* (1921).

[32] See his letter to Mr. Maurice, January 16, 1851 (already quoted), in *Charles Kingsley, Letters and Memories of His Life*, ed. by his wife, abr. from London ed., *Scribner's*, 1894.

[33] Author's *Note to the Reader.*

[34] *Walter Pater, a Critical Study*, by Edward Thomas, N. Y., 1913.

[35] Mr. F. S. Dunn, while speaking with due reverence of Pater's chaste diction and chaster ethics, notes two trifling errors made in *Marius the Epicurean* in regard to the topography of Rome. (F. S. Dunn, *The Historical Novel in the Classroom,—Classical Journal*, April, 1911.)

[36] Quinton in *The Money God*, had spoken of the two favorite bears of the Emperor Galerius, giving as his source Lactantius, *de Morte persecutorum*, cap. 21.

Bibliography

Explanation

The following list of titles will be divided into sections, according to the plan followed in tracing the development of the novel of Roman life, and is intended to serve as a supplement to Section III of the foregoing study. In each section of the list the titles will be arranged, as nearly as possible, according to the chronological order of the dates of publication, except in cases where an author has written more than one fiction on Roman life. In such cases all his books will be mentioned together in the order of their publication. In case the original date of publication of a book is uncertain, the date of the best available edition will be given; or if no date is known for a book, it will be listed at the end of the section in which it belongs, or after other books, (the date of which is known), by the same author. In some cases title will be listed of books which are out of print but may be found here and there in public libraries. Books which I believe are practically unobtainable will be marked with an asterisk (*). The list includes all true English novels of Roman life, as well as all other books written in English, whose titles have been collected as by-products of the novel of Roman life. These by-products will be classified according to their relative importance to the study of the novel of Roman life, the more important books being given first.

The earliest known date of each novel is given in parentheses, (). Short stories, including those published in collections, have been omitted.

Novels of Roman Life, and Their By-Products

1. Novels Connected with the Genesis of the Novel of Roman Life.

Letters Supposed to have passed between Theodosius and Constantia—Langhorne, John; London, (1778).

Zenobia, Queen of Palmyra, a Narrative Founded on History—Miss O'Keefe; London, (1814).

Valerius, a Roman Story—Lockhart, J. G.; London, (1821)—N. Y. Harper, 1835.

The Epicurean—Moore, Thomas; (1827)—McClurg, Chicago, 1890.

Salathiel, the Immortal—Croly, George; (1827)—Repub. Funk & Wagnalls, New York, under title, *Tarry Thou Till I Come*, 1903.

The Alexandrians, an Egyptian Tale of the Fourth Century—Anon. Whittaker, London, (1830).

The Last Days of Pompeii—Bulwer-Lytton, Sir E. G.; Dutton, N. Y., (1834).

The Stoic—Stanford, Jane K.; London, (1834).

2. IMPORTANT NOVELS BY PREACHERS.

Zenobia, or the Fall of Palmyra—Ware, William; Burt, N. Y., (1836)—James Miller, N. Y., 1869.

Aurelian: Rome, Third Century—Ware, William; orig. pub. as *Probus*, (1838)—Burt, N. Y., n. d., under title of *Aurelian*.

Julian; Scenes in Judea—Ware, William; Estes, Boston, (1841).

Hypatia—Kingsley, Charles; (1853)—MacMillan, N. Y., 1902.

Fabiola: The Church of the Catacombs—Wiseman, Cardinal N.; Burns & Oates, London, (1855).

Callista—Newman, Cardinal John Henry; (1856)—Longman, N. Y., 1890.

Darkness and Dawn—Farrar, Archdeacon Frederic W.; (1892)—Longmans, N. Y., 1895.

Gathering Clouds—Farrar, Archdeacon Frederic W.; (1895)—Longmans, N. Y., 1896.

Perpetua—Baring-Gould, Rev. S.; Dutton, N. Y., (1897).

Domitia—Baring-Gould; Fred A. Stokes, N. Y., (1898).

3. TWO NOVELS BY PEDANTS.

Dion and the Sibyls, a Romance of the First Century—Keon, Miles Gerald; London, Bentley, (1866).

The Money God, or The Empire and the Papacy—Quinton, M. A.; Kelly, Piet & Co., Baltimore (1873).

(**Aurelia, or the Jews of Capena Gate*—Quinton, M. A.; n. d.)

(**Furius, a Tale of the Early Christians at Rome*—Quinton, M. A.; n. d.)

4. IMPORTANT NOVELS BY TEACHERS.

Helena's Household; Rome, First Century—De Mille, James; (1858)—Ward & Drummond, N. Y., 1897.

*The Martyr of the Catacombs—De Mille, James; (1858).

Kallistratus, an Autobiography—Gilkes, A. H.; Longmans, (1897)—Frowde, London, 1912.

*Four Sons—Gilkes, A. H.; Symcox, Dulwich, (1909).

A Friend of Caesar—Davis, William Stearns; Macmillan, N. Y., (1900).

The Unwilling Vestal—White, Edward Lucas; Dutton, N. Y., (1918).

Andivius Hedulio—White, Edward Lucas; Dutton, N. Y., (1921).

*Claudian, Second Century—Munro, Rev. Edward M., M. A.; Masters, London, n. d.

5. ARTISTIC NOVELS OF ROMAN LIFE.

*The Fawn of Sertorius—Landor, Robert Eyres; Longmans, London, (1846); (scene in Spain).

Marius, the Epicurean—Pater, Walter Horatio; Macmillan, N. Y., (1885).

Veranilda—Gissing, George; Archibald, Constable & Co., London, (1904).

Evander—Phillpotts, Eden; Macmillan, N. Y., (1919).

Pan and the Twins—Phillpotts, Eden; Macmillan, N. Y., (1922).

6. POPULAR NOVELS OF ROMAN LIFE, INCLUDING THOSE NOT OTHERWISE CLASSIFIED.

*The Empress—Bennett, G.; Smith & Elder, London, (1835); (listed as a novel of Roman life).

Attila, or the Huns—James, G. P. R.; (1837)—Routledge, London, 1903.

*The Gladiator, a Tale of the Roman Empire—Lamont, Miss M. M.; (1840)—Longmans, London, 1849.

Julia of Baiae; or The Days of Nero—Pickering, Ellen; Saxton & Miles, N. Y., (1843).

Antonina—Collins, Wilkie; Harper, N. Y., (1850).

The Siege of Damascus, a Historical Romance—Nisbet, James; Chapman, London, (1851).

The Roman Traitor, or the Days of Cicero, Cato and Catiline—Herbert, H. W.; Peterson, Philadelphia, (1853).

The Wager of Battle—Herbert, H. W., n. d. (Roman Britain).

The Slaves of Sabinus, Jew and Gentile—Yonge, Charlotte M.; National Society's Depository, Sanctuary, Westminster, (1861)—Whittaker, N. Y., 1890.

The Cook and the Captive; or Attalus the Hostage—Yonge, Charlotte M.; Whittaker, N. Y., (1894).

The Gladiators—Whyte-Melville, G. J.; (1863)—Ward & Lock, N. Y., 1890.

Ænone, a Tale of Slave Life in Rome—Kip, L.; Bradburn, N. Y.; (1866).

Ierne of Armorica; a Tale of the Time of Clovis—Bateman, J. C.; Sadlier, N. Y., (1873), (scene in Gaul).

Claudius Causton, Mrs. R. K.; Hatchards, London, (1878).

Blue and Green—Pottinger, Sir Henry; Chapman, London, (1879).

Ben Hur—Wallace, Gen. Lew; Harper, N. Y., (1880).

Neaera—Graham, John W.; Macmillan, N. Y., (1886).

The Son of a Star—Richardson, B. W.; Longmans, N. Y., (1888).

Masters of the World—Hoppus, Mary A. M.; Bentley, (1888), (the date 1885 is probably incorrect).

A Queen Among Queens—MacDowall, C. J. F. S.; Swan, London, (1889), (Zenobia).

Cleopatra—Haggard, Sir H. Rider; Longmans, N. Y., (1889).

Pearl-Maiden—Haggard, Sir H. Rider; Longmans, London, (1902).

Acte—Westbury, Hugh, pseud., (Farrie, Hugh C.); Bentley, London, (1890).

Barabbas—Corelli, Marie; Lippincott, Philadelphia, (1893).

The Sign of the Cross—Barrett, Wilson; Lippincott, Philadelphia, (1897).

Pharos, the Egyptian—Boothby, G.; Ward & Lock, London, (1899).

The Lion's Brood—Osborne, Duffield; Doubleday, N. Y., (1901).

She Stands Alone—Ashton, Mark; L. C. Page & Co., Boston, (1901).

Amor Victor—Kenyon, Orr; Stokes, N. Y., (3rd ed., 1902).

Vergilius, a Tale of the Coming of Christ—Bacheller, Irving; Harper, N. Y., (1904).

Lux Crucis, a Tale of the Great Apostle—Gardenhire, S. M.; Harper, N. Y., (1904).

**Marcus and Faustina*—Carrel, Frederic; J. Long, London, (1904).

**Et tu, Sejane*—Twells, Miss J. H.; Coates, Philadelphia, (1904).

Psyche—Cramp, Walter S.; Little & Brown, Boston, (1905).

An Heir to Empire—Cramp, Walter S.; Richard C. Badger, The Gorham Press, Boston, (1913).

**The Son of the Swordmaker*—Reed, Opie; Laird, Chicago, (1906).

Under Pontius Pilate—Schuyler, William; Funk & Wagnalls, N. Y., (1906).

Saul of Tarsus—Miller, Elizabeth; Bobbs-Merrill Co., Indianapolis, (1906).

The City of Delight, a Love Drama of the Siege and Fall of Jerusalem—Miller, Elizabeth; Bobbs-Merrill Co., Indianapolis, (1908).

**The Senator Licinius*—Kelly, W. P.; Dutton, N. Y., (1909).

*The Doomed City—Carling, J. R.; Ward & Lock, London, (1910).

The Fetters of Freedom—Brady, Cyrus Townsend; Dodd, Mead & Co., N. Y., (1913).

Unto Caesar—Orczy, Baroness; Doran, N. Y., (1914).

The Standard Bearer—Whitehead, A. C.; American Book Co., N. Y., (1915).

Behold the Woman—Harré, T. Everett; Lippincott, Philadelphia, (1916).

Princess Salome—Jenkins, B. A.; Lippincott, Philadelphia, (1921).

Revelation—Deamer, Dulcie; Boni & Liveright, N. Y., (1922).

Nabala—Caskie, Jaquelin A.; J. B. Bell, Inc., Lynchburg, Va., (1922).

7. BOOKS FOR BOYS, INCLUDING MOST BOOKS ON ROMAN BRITAIN.

Two Thousand Years Ago—Church, Rev. A. J.; Dodd, Mead & Co., N. Y., (1885).

The Count of the Saxon Shore—Church, Rev. A. J.; Putnam, N. Y., (1887), (Britain).

To the Lions—Church, Rev. A. J.; Putnam, N. Y., (1889).

The Burning of Rome—Church, Rev. A. J.; (1892)—Macmillan, N. Y., 1902.

Lords of the World—Church, Rev. A. J.; Scribner, N. Y., (1898).

The Crown of Pine—Church, Rev. A. J.; Seely, London, (1905)—Scribners, N. Y., 1906.

**No. XIII; or The Story of the Lost Vestal*—Marshall, E.; Cassell, London, (1885), (Britain).

The Young Carthaginian—Henty, G. A.; Burt, N. Y., (1886).

For the Temple—Henty, G. A.; Blackie, London, (1888).

Beric, the Briton—Henty, G. A.; Scribners, N. Y., (1892)—Scribners, N. Y., 1911, (Britain).

**One Traveller Returns*—Murray, D. C., & Herman, H.; Chatto, London, (1887), (Britain).

The Wonderful Adventures of Phra the Phoenician—Arnold, Edwin Lester; Burt, N. Y., (1890), (Britain).

Lepidus the Centurion, a Roman of To-day—Arnold, E. L.; Crowell, N. Y., (1901), (a Roman brought back to life in England).

**Woe to the Conquered*—Clark, Alfred; Low, London, (1893).

**A Duke of Britain*—Maxwell, Sir H. E.; Blackwood, (1895).

**Aneroestes the Gaul*—Smith, E. M.; Unwin, London, (1899).

**Britain's Greatness Foretold*—"Trevelyan, Marie"; Hogg, London, (1900).

**A Story of Ancient Wales*—Elrington, H.; Whittaker, N. Y., (1900).

**Marcus, the Young Centurion*—Fenn, G. M.; Nister, London, (1904).

A Daughter of the Druids—Sedgwick, S. N.; Stockwell, (1904), (Britain).

*At Sunrise—Spurell, Herbert; Greening, London, (1904), (Britain).

Nikanor, Teller of Tales—Taylor, C. B.; McClurg, Chicago, (1906), (Britain).

Under the Roman Eagles—"Sagon, Amyot"; Partridge, London, (1907).

The Meeting of the Ways—Baxter, J. D.; Greening, London, (1908), (Britain).

Durobrivae; Roman Rochester—Harris, E.; Harris, Rochester, (1909).

*Boudicca—Ward, C. H. D.; Ousely, London, (1912), (Britain).

8. STORIES OF RELIGIOUS INSTRUCTION.

Explanation of Abbreviations:

R. T. S.—Religious Tract Society, London.

S. P. C. K.—Society for Promoting Christian Knowledge, London.

Naomi: or the Last Days of Jerusalem—Webb, Mrs. J. B. Peploe; Routledge, London, (1841), (date 1840 is probably incorrect).

Julamerk: a Tale of the Nestorians—Webb, J. B. P.; Ward & Lock, London, (1848).

The Martyrs of Carthage—Webb, J. B. P.; Ward & Lock, London, (1850).

Alypius of Tagaste—Webb, J. B. P.; R. T. S., (Revell, N. Y.), (1865).

*Pomponia; the Gospel in Caesar's Household—Webb, J. B. P.; Pres. Pub. Co., Philadelphia, (1867).

*Evadne: or An Empire in Its Fall—Rowcroft, C.; Boone, London, (1850).

The Egyptian Wanderers—Neale, Rev. John Mason; S. P. C. K., (1854).

*The Farm of Aptonga—Neale, J. M.; Parker, London, (1856)—S. P. C. K., 1918.

*The Exiles of the Cebenna—Neale, J. M., (pseud. Aurelius Gratianus); Parker, London, (1859)—S. P. C. K., 1918.

The Quay of the Dioscuri—Neale, J. M.; S. P. C. K., (1917).

The Lions of Wady-Arabia—Neale, J. M.; S. P. C. K., (1917).

The Prince of the House of David; or Three Years in the Holy City—Ingraham, Rev. J. H.; (1855)—Roberts, Boston, (1895).

*Adonijah; the Jewish Dispersion—Strickland, Jane M.; Simpkin, London, (1856).

*Parthenia, or the Last Days of Paganism—Lee, Mrs. E. B.; Routledge, London, (1858).

Caecilia Metella, or Rome Enslaved—"Julia, Aemilia," (Emily Julia Black); Chapman, London, (1859).

Claudia and Pudens: Early Christians in Gloucester—Lysons, S.; Hamilton, London, (1861).

*The Villa of Claudius—Cutts, Rev. E. L.; S. P. C. K., (1861).

Martyrs of Spain—Charles, Mrs. Elizabeth Rundle; S. P. C. K., (1862).

The Victory of the Vanquished—Charles, E. R.; Dodd, Mead & Co., N. Y., (1871).

Conquering and to Conquer—Charles, E. R.; S. P. C. K., (1876)—Dodd, Mead & Co., N. Y., (1876).

Lapsed, But Not Lost—Charles, E. R.; S. P. C. K., (1877)—Dodd, Mead & Co., N. Y., (1879).

Attila, and His Conquerors—Charles, E. R.; S. P. C. K., (1894).

*Life in Judea; or Glimpses of the First Christian Age—Richards, Maria T.; Simpkin, London, (1862).

*Victor, a Tale of the Great Persecution—Perry, G. G.; S. P. C. K., London, (1864).

*Vestina's Martyrdom—Pitman, Emma R.; Hodder, London, (1869).

Claudia—Tucker, Charlotte; Nelson, London, (1869).

Freedom, a Tale of the Early Christians—Tucker, C.; R. T. S., (1871).

Daybreak in Britain—Tucker, C., (pseud. A. L. O. E.); R. T. S., (1880).

Stars in a Stormy Night, or Light from the Catacombs—"E. L. M."; Nelson, London, (1870).

Æmilius: Decian and Valerian Persecutions—Crake, Rev. A. D.; Mowbray, London, (1871).

Evanus; Constantine the Great—Crake, A. D.; Mowbray, London, (1872).

The Camp on the Severn—Crake, A. D.; Mowbray, London, (1875)—The Vatican Library, N. Y., 1891.

The Victor's Laurel—Crake, A. D.; Mowbray, London, (1885)—The Vatican Library, N. Y., 1889.

*The Standard Bearer—Palmer, Ellen; Hamilton, Edinburgh, (1871).

*Nonna: A Story of the Days of Julian the Apostate—Palmer, Ellen; Hamilton, Edinburgh, (1872).

Marcella of Rome, (also called *The Fearless Christian Maiden*)—Knevels, Mrs. C. D., (pseud. Eastwood, Frances); Shaw, London, (1872).

**Adah, the Jewish Maiden*—Gray, Agnes M.; Hamilton, Edinburgh, (1872).

*Cyllene—Sneyd, Henry; Longmans, London, (1873).

*Epiphanius—Mossman, T. W.; Hayes, London, (1874).

Gaudentius—Davies, Rev. G. S.; S. P. C. K., (1874).

Julian's Dream—Davies, G. S.; S. P. C. K., (1875).

St. Paul in Greece—Davies, G. S., n. d.

Glaucia: the Greek Slave—Leslie, Emma; Nelson and Phillips, N. Y., (1874)—R. T. S., 1904.

Quadratus, a Tale of the World in the Church—Leslie, E.; Phillips and Hunt, Cincinnati, (1875).

Sowing Beside All Waters, a Tale of the Early Church—Leslie, E.; R. T. S., n. d. (This is merely *Quadratus* rewritten.)

Flavia—Leslie, E.; Nelson and Phillips, N. Y., (1875), later published under the title of

Out of the Mouth of the Lion; or the Church in the Catacombs—Leslie, E.; Bradley, Boston, (1880), (also pub. anon.).

On the Emperor's Service—Leslie, E.; R. T. S., (1904).

*Edol the Druid—Kingston, W. H. G.; Partridge, London, (1874).

**Jovinian; Early Days of Papal Rome*—Kingston, W. H. G.; Hamilton, London, (1877).

Zipporah, the Jewish Maiden—Brewsher, Mrs. M. E.; London, (1875).

Philochristus—Abbott, Rev. Edwin A.; Macmillan, N. Y., (1878).

Onesimus, Christ's Freedman: Memoirs of a Disciple of St. Paul—Abbott, E. A.; Revell, N. Y., (1882)—(Repub. Corwin, C. E., ed.)

Silanus the Christian—Abbott, E. A.; Macmillan, N. Y., (1906).

*Narcissus—Carpenter, Rev. W. Boyd; S. P. C. K., (Young, N. Y.), (1879).

*Dio the Athenian—Burr, E. F.; Methodist Bk., N. Y., (1880).

**Aleph the Chaldean; the Messiah as Seen from Alexandria*—Burr, E. F.; Ketcham, N. Y., (1891).

Fabius, the Roman—Burr, E. F.; Baker, N. Y., n. d.

The Wards of Plotinus—Hunt, Mrs. John; Strahan, London, (1881).

Valeria, or the Martyr of the Catacombs—Witherow, W. H.; Woolmer, London, (1883).

Dorcas, the Daughter of Faustina—Kouns, Nathan C.; Fords, N. Y., (1884).

Arius the Libyan: an Idyl of the Primitive Church—Kouns, N. C.; Appleton, N. Y., (1884).

From Crown to Crown; a Tale of the Early Church—Anon.; Hatchards, London, (1885).

By the King and Queen—Mercier, Mrs. Jerome; Rivington, London, (1886).

The Slave Girl of Pompeii—Holt, Emily S.; Shaw, London, (1886).

Flora, the Roman Martyr—Anon.; Burns & Oates, London, (1886)—Benziger, N. Y., 1887.

Leah of Jerusalem—Berry, E. P.; Randolph & Co., (1890).

Philip—Cutler, Mary C.; Nelson, London, (1890).

A Son of Isaachar—Brooks, S.; Putnam, N. Y., (1890).

Come Forth—Ward, Mrs. Elizabeth Phelps; (1890), (story of Lazarus).

The Doom of the Holy City—Farmer, Lydia H.; Randolph, N. Y., (1895).

Titus, A Comrade of the Cross—Kingsley, Florence M.; D. C. Cook, Chicago, (1895).

Stephen, a Soldier of the Cross—Kingsley, F. M.; Henry Altemus, Philadelphia, (1896).

Paul, a Herald of the Cross—Kingsley, F. M.; Altemus, Philadelphia, (1897).

The Cross Triumphant—Kingsley, F. M.; Ward & Lock, London, (1900).

Tor, a Street Boy of Jerusalem—Kingsley, F. M.; D. C. Cook, Chicago, (1905).

Veronica—Kingsley, F. M., Appleton, N. Y., (1913).

The Story of the Other Wise Man—VanDyke, Henry J.; Harper, N. Y., (1895)—Harper, N. Y., 1907.

Antipas, Son of Chusa, and Others Whom Jesus Loved—Houghton, Louise S.; Randolph, N. Y., (1896).

John, a Tale of King Messiah—Woods, Katherine P.; Dodd, Mead & Co., N. Y., (1896).

The Son of Ingar—Woods, Katherine P.; Dodd, Mead & Co., N. Y., (1897).

From Dusk to Dawn—Woods, K. P.; Appleton, N. Y., (1899).

*Victor Serenus—Wood, Henry; Gay & Bird, London, (1898).

The Victory that Overcometh—Gee, Annie L.; S. P. C. K., (1898).

The Minister of Carthage—Mason, Caroline Atwater; Doubleday, Garden City, N. Y., (1899).

The White Shield—Mason, C. A.; Griffith & Rowland, Philadelphia, (1904).

Paul of Tarsus—Bird, Robert; Nelson, London, (1900).

Lucius Flavus—Spillman, Rev. Joseph; Kilner, Philadelphia, (1900).

Diomede the Centurion—Henderson, Rev. H. A.; Methodist Bk., N. Y., (1902).

*Adnah—Ellis, J. Breckenridge; R. T. S., (1902).

*Sancta Paula—Perry, W. C.; Sonnenschein, London, (1902).

Bethsaida—Dearborn, Malcolm; Dillingham, N. Y., (1902).

*In Holiest Troth—Fidelis, Sister Mary; Burns & Oates, London, (1903).

**A Hero in Wolf-skin*—Bevan, Tom; R. T. S., (1904).

**The Court of Pilate*—Hobbs, Roe R.; Fenno, N. Y., (1906).

**The Story of a Child That Jesus Took*—Smyth, S. P. N.; Pilgrim Press, Boston, (1907).

*Nizra—Klarman, Andrew; Fred. Pustet & Co., (1908).

**Leo of Mediolanum*—Hollis, Gertrude; S. P. C. K., (1909).

**For Queen and Emperor*—Protheroe, Ernest; R. T. S., (1909).

**The Forgotten Door*—Cowper, Frank; S. P. C. K., (1909).

Mary of Magdala—Roberson, Mrs. H. G.; Saalfield, Akron, O., (1909).

Mary of Magdala—Saltus, Edgar; Greening, London, (1909).

**The Testament of Judas*—Byatt, H.; Long, London, (1909).

Prisca of Patmos—McCook, Rev. Henry C.; The Westminster Press, Philadelphia, (1911).

Faustula—"Ayscough, John", (Francis Browning Drew); Chatto, London, (Kilner, Philadelphia), (1912).

The Story of Phaedrus; How We Got the Greatest Book in the World—Hillis, Rev. Newell Dwight; Macmillan, N. Y., (1914).

The Coming of the King—Babcock, Bernie; Bobbs Merrill Co., Indianapolis, (1921).

Simon of Cyrene—Shastid, Thomas Hall; Wahr, Ann Arbor, Michigan, (1923).

9. BOOKS LISTED AS NOVELS OF ROMAN LIFE. (Date of Publication Uncertain.)

1st Century.

Iola, the Senator's Daughter—Hillhouse, N. L.

Julia of Baiae—Brown, J. W.; n. d., (possibly a forgery from Ellen Pickering's novel of the same title).

Philo, Life in the First Century—Hamilton, J.

Unlaid Ghost: a Study in Metempsychosis—Anon.

Vergilia—Grey, G.

2nd Century.

Letters from Rome—Wace, Eustace.

Marius Flaminius; the Days of Hadrian—Anon.

3rd Century.

The Theban Legion—Blackburn, E. M.

10. RELIGIOUS STORIES. (Date of Publication Uncertain.)

a. Those with Scene near Rome.

1st Century.

Mina: The Days of Nero and the Early Christians—Ross, Andrew.

Neither Rome nor Judea—Hoven, E.

2nd Century.

*The Child Martyr and Early Christians in Rome—Anon.
*Three Roman Girls—Bamford, M. E.; American Baptist Pub. Co.
*The Three Berenices—Bright, Mrs. A. M.

The Captive Maiden—Anon.

4th Century.

The Last Battle of the Gods—Kelly, F. C.; Philadelphia.

b. Those with Scene in Africa.

African Fabiola, or The Church of Carthage in the Days of Tertullian—Clarke, A. C.
Fabiola's Sisters, a Companion to Fabiola—Clarke, A. C.
*Deodatus; or Martyr of Carthage—Williams, E.
*Our Little Carthaginian Cousin—Winslow, Clara V.
*Vandal, or Half a Christian—Luby, William J.

c. Those with Scene in Asia.

Andros of Ephesus—Copus, Rev. J. E.
The Son of Siro—Copus, Rev. J. E.; Benziger, N. Y.
*Aslane: Manners of the Nestorian Christians—Anon.
The Fall of Palmyra, Rome, and the Early Christians—Anon.
*The Fall of Damascus—Russell, C. W.

d. Those with Scene in Palestine.
1st Century.

Judea Capta—Toner, C. E.
**The Jews' Tragedy*—Heming.
**Zerah, the Believing Jew*—Anon.

After 1st Century.

Abdiel; a Tale of the Early Christians—Anon.

e. Those with Scene in Britain.

*Mona the Vestal—Dorsey, Anna H.; Lippincott, Philadelphia, c. 1850.
**The Alleluia Battle, or Pelagianism in Britain*—Anon.
*The Druidess—Anon.